D1308643

Larry L. Vantine

TEACHING AMERICAN INDIAN HISTORY: AN INTERDISCIPLINARY APPROACH

San Francisco, California
1978

E
76
.6
.V36

Published by
R&E RESEARCH ASSOCIATES, INC.
4843 Mission Street
San Francisco, California 94112
Publishers
Robert D. Reed and Adam S. Eterovich

Library of Congress Card Catalog Number
78-62223

I.S.B.N.

0-88247-546-0

COPYRIGHT 1978

by

LARRY L. VANTINE

JACKSONVILLE UNIVERSITY LIBRARY

203618

TABLE OF CONTENTS

Teaching American Indian History: An Interdisciplinary Approach

In 1971, Wilcomb Washburn, a prominent historian of American Indians, commenting on the problems that confront the writing of American Indian history, wrote, "The first and greatest problem concerns the possibility of writing a good general history of the American Indian. I think it fair to say that no historian has yet succeeded in producing an unchallengeable model."[1] Today, this statement still holds true.[2]

Many reasons can be cited why historians have not succeeded in the task. It has been widely accepted that the study of the American Indians, in both its cultural and historical context, is the responsibility of anthropologists, and in more recent times, sociologists. Justification for assigning this responsibility was often based on the assumption that anthropologists were better prepared for studying "primitive societies." For this reason, history departments had not moved to establish concern in the field and often discouraged young historians from going into it. While anthropologists have come closest in producing an outstanding general history of the American Indian, they too have not completely solved the problem.

The necessity of an interdisciplinary approach in writing and teaching American Indian history can be seen in contrasting the focus of two representative works in the field, by an anthropologist and an historian. Edward Spicer, an anthropologist, in writing A Short History of the Indians of the United States, focuses on the internal relations of Indian tribes and discusses subsequent white relations in terms of culture change and persistence. This theme of culture change in writing American Indian history focuses on revitalization movements, assimilative and acculturation efforts, and Pan-Indian movements. The failure of government programs and conflicts between white and Indian are explained by differences arising from two diverse value systems, that of the Indian and that of the European. Indian-Indian relations are an important aspect of the anthropological approach. The representative text written by a historian is Angie Debo's <u>A History of the Indians of the United States</u>. Like most related works by historians, the book focuses primarily on Indian-white relations. The focus is more external as opposed to internal. This is reflected in the titles of several chapters: "The White Man Comes", "The White Man Stays", and "The White Man Repents". While sympathetic to the Indian's view, it nevertheless ignores the internal dynamics of Indian life and politics. Robert Berkhofer Jr. comments on the shortcomings of Indian-white histories:

> Even when the historian thought he was portraying the Indian "side" in his writing, he adopted implicitly either the white view of his sources or, equally invidious, the assumption that the outcome of his story is determined more by the white side than by the Indian side. Regardless of the reason, the historian continued to concentrate upon the white "side" of the story even when he professed to be describing the Indian viewpoint. In brief, the historian treated Indians as passive objects responding to white stimuli rather than as individuals coping creatively in a variety of ways with the different situations in which they found themselves.[3]

> For historians, whites were the main actors; for anthropologists, Indian culture or society was the center of attention.[4]

What is needed, as shown by these two examples, is a fusion of both perspectives. While the central focus should certainly be on internal relations, with culture change and persistence as a theme, the aspect of Indian-white relations should not be sacrificed. An impartial treatment of Indian-white relations goes far in dispelling stereotyped images of the Indian and gives a sense of balance to the usual one-sided perspective of most United States histories. A grasp of the political and social history of the United States is necessary for a better understanding of the dictates of Indian policy during particular periods and the attitudes of whites toward the Indian.

The argument for an interdisciplinary approach in writing American Indian history has been advanced by several outstanding writers in the field. In this regard,

Wilcomb Washburn, Wilbur Jacobs and Robert Berkhofer Jr. are the foremost historians. The anthropologists are represented by Edward Spicer and John Ewers. With the exception of Spicer, anthropologists have tended not to write general histories on American Indians but concentrate their efforts on tribal histories in a particular ethnographic area.

The answer, then, to writing and teaching American Indian history is an interdisciplinary approach. This is hopefully what my project will accomplish. As a teaching unit on American Indians, embodying both historical and cultural material, it could become a guide to writing an acceptable general history of the American Indian.

Thus my project attempts to furnish an interdisciplinary approach, anthropological and historical, to the teaching of American Indian history. This is reflected in learning objectives, outlines, activities, and resources. It provides the instructor with a viable framework focusing on activities and instructional objectives which are "value-oriented".[5]

Since the interdisciplinary approach focuses on culture change as the underlying theme for teaching and writing American Indian history, consideration of American Indian values, their cultural relativity, and their comparison with Euro-American concepts are essential. Using such an approach, conflicts between whites and Indians can be explained, in part, by differences in cultural values. An inventory of those values held by both groups allows the student to better understand what specific values American Indian policy attempted to change, reasons or justification for the direct changes, and why most of the programs consequently failed to accomplish their objectives.

"Values are concepts. . .Like all concepts, they do not exist in experience but in the minds of men. They represent the quality of worth or merit on which men place various aspects of their experience."[6] One area of values which is important in the study of American Indian history is ethics. "Ethics refers to the study and justifi-

3

cation of conduct---how men act. At the base of the study of ethics is the question of morals---the reflective consideration of what is right and wrong."[7]

Thus, material should reflect a concern for building foundations on which students can justify their reasoning in response to questions of whether a particular policy or attitude directed toward the Indian is justifiable. For example, was the Battle of Wounded Knee really a "battle" or a "massacre". Can the action taken by the 7th Cavalry by justified? Value-oriented questions ask students to reason or justify the conduct of peoples in their relations with other peoples.

Explanation of Categories Used in Teaching Units

Objectives

Instructional objectives should specify as clearly as possible the kinds of behaviors desired of students and the content they will be expected to learn.[8] In addition, the objectives serve to function as a guide for writing evaluations.[9] By combining two or more objectives or applying a specific objective to an example, the instructor can construct excellent evaluation questions. Included in the appendix are evaluations I have used in classes which might prove to be helpful. Please, remember that the objectives listed are drawn from a number of sources.[10] Thus the instructors might find it necessary to select those objectives which apply to their textbook and classroom material. (However, since an interdisciplinary approach is being utilized, materials should be used, either lecture, textbook, or supplemental readins, which cover a majority of the objectives.)

Outline

The function of the outline is to serve as a guide for the selection and organization of subject matter. The tribe(s) used in the case studies will depend on the textbook(s) being used or the instructor's preference. Many times, for example, the units on contemporary affairs, or Indian cultures west of the Mississippi, the outline may be broken down into its component parts (I, II, III, etc.)

and used individually as a teaching unit.

Points to Emphasize

This category provides, as the title indicates, important points which should be emphasized, especially if the material in class overlooks them.

Activities

I have constructed a variety of activities, i.e., map assignments, oral and written reports, panel discussions, and charts of use in the classroom. A majority of activities are structured to allow students to analyze, synthesize, and finally judge or evaluate the material presented, thus reaching beyond the more mundane technique of who is or what is. Students should be allowed to present their opinions, but also called upon to support them.

Instructional Aids

I have collected and compiled under this category a variety of instructional aid material for the classroom. Consult the appropriate film catalogs or distributors for a more detailed description of the materials. Explanation of citations: Type of instructional aid: Title (subject of aid if not apparent by title) (Distributors, producer, and/or rental agencies).

Student and Teacher Resources

The division between the two categories are determined by reading and comprehension level of the material. Student and teacher resources cited in the introductory units on American Indian culture and history serve as the bibliography for sources quoted in their succeeding units. Teacher resources are identified by an asterisk (*).

FOOTNOTES

[1]Wilcomb Washburn, "The Writing of American Indian History: A Status Report, Pacific Historical Review, August, 1971, p. 262.

[2]The rationalization for an interdisciplinary approach in writing American Indian history is being used in this paper as common ground for an interdisciplinary approach in teaching the subject.

[3]Robert F. Berkhofer Jr. "The Political Context of a New Indian History," Pacific Historical Review (August, 1971), p. 364.

[4]Ibid. p. 359.

[5]Jack Fraenkel, Helping Students Think and Value: Strategies for Teaching the Social Studies (Englewood Cliffs, NJ: Prentice-Hall, Inc., 1973).

[6]Ibid. p. 231.

[7]Ibid. pp. 231-232.

[8]Ibid. p. 10.

[9]Ibid. chapters 2 and 7.

[10]Primarily Debo's A History of the Indians of the United States and Spicer's A Short History of the Indians of the United States.

UNIT ONE

What (or Who) is an Indian?

Objectives

At the conclusion of this unit, the student will be able to:

Identify: "enrolled Indian"
            "non-enrolled Indian"

Compare and contrast the various factors used in defining "Indian"

Differentiate the categories used by various government agencies and tribal groups in establishing Indian identity

Judge the validity of the numerous and diverse definitions of an "Indian"

Outline

I.   MAIN CATEGORIES USED IN DEFINING "INDIAN"

    A.   Racial
        1. Based on quantum of "Indian" blood

    B.   Cultural
        1. Emphasis on cultural factors
            a. Use of common language or dialect
            b. Similar customs and religious beliefs

    C.   Social
        1. ". . .people who have some degree of Indian blood (usually less rather than more) and some (often fleeting) familiarity with their culture heritage but who are in terms of either race or culture only marginally 'Indians' (Svensson 1973:6)"

Points to Emphasize

The United States government and the Indians often differ on the emphasis of criteria used in considering who is an Indian.

Traditionally, Indians identified themselves in terms of kinship and tribal affiliations.

Since the earliest years of contact between Indians and Europenas in the New World, there has been a constant and relatively large-scale degree of "mixing" between Indians and others (Svensson 1973:2).

Urban Indians and reservation Indians differ as to the definition of Indian in terms of qualifying for government services.

Even tribal governments differ in their criteria for qualifying as a tribal member.

The category used for defining "Indian" depends on who is asking and for what purposes.

Activities

Present class with a definition of "American Indian" from a standard dictionary and discuss.

Discuss the background of important "mixed-blood" Indian leaders, i.e., John Ross, Quanah Parker, then confront class with the question "Were they Indian or white?" What criteria are you using for your answer? This might also be done with mixed-bloods or captives who were assimilated.

Discuss Svensson's conclusion that "At its heart, Indianess is a state of being, a cast of mind, a relationship to the Universe. It is undefinable." (Svensson 1973:9)

Instructional Aids

Student and Teacher Resources

Owl, Frell M.
    1962 Who or What is an American Indian? (Ethnohistory, v.9).

Svensson, Francis
    1973 The Ethnics in American Politics: American Indians
        (Long Island, New York: Burgess Publishing Co.)
        (see chapted titled "What is an Indian")

INTRODUCTION TO UNITS ON AMERICAN INDIAN CULTURES

General Objectives

At the end of the units on North American Indian cultures, the student will be able to:

Locate specified tribes in North America, in the past and present

Summarize the cultural background of selected North American Indian tribes

Compare and contrast selected tribes in the following areas: (1) subsistence patterns; (2) settlement patterns; (3) material culture; (4) political organization; (5) social organization; (6) religion; (7) the arts (usually optional). For a further breakdown of these categories see page 17.

Compare and contrast American Indian tribes overall in the areas listed above

Compare and contrast Euro-American concepts to American Indian values in the following areas: (1) land tenure; (2) government-political organization; (3) religion and (4) social organization

Evaluate (judge) a culture according to its own standards and values (cultural relativism)

Define and apply selected anthropological terms used in the study of American Indian cultures

Criticize the conept of ethnocentricity

Criticize the image of the "stereotyped" Indian

Outline

I.   CLASSIFICATION SCHEMES

     A.   Culture areas
     B.   Language groups

II. SURVEY OF NORTH AMERICAN INDIAN TRIBES: LOCATION AND POPULATION

     A.   Pre-Columbian
     B.   Present

Points to Emphasize

Diversity of Indian cultures, even within the same culture area.

The relationship of American Indian cultures and their respective physical environments. The strongest influence of environment is exerted on subsistence patterns and material culture but also affects the areas of political organization, social organization, and religion.

Diversity of Indian languages. No such thing as speaking "Indian".

The study of intertribal relations between tribes in areas of trade, diplomacy and warfare.

North American Indian cultures were not static but dynamic.

Indian cultures throughout North America were highly developed by the time the first Europeans arrived.

Indian languages were fully developed with thousands of words and precise systems of prononciation and grammar.

Activities

Oral report on an American Indian tribe. (Note - Tribes chosen for presentation should not include those considered by instructor or textbook since the objective of this activity is to familiarize students with the greatest number of Indian tribes possible.) (See pages 18 - 19 for suggested format.)

Instructional Aids

Handout of anthropological terms used in the study of North American Indians (see pages 16-17 for suggested format).

Maps:
    (1) Distribution of American Indian tribes at time of European contact
    (2) Current location of American Indian reservations
    (3) Cultural areas of North America
    (4) Language groups, North American Indians

    The following maps show one or more of the above:
    North America Before Columbus/Indians of North America (NGS)
    American Indians (CES)
    Indian Tribes and Settlements in the New World, 1500-1750 (Nystrom)
    Indian Land Areas (BIA)

Films: Indians of Early America (EBEC; Berkeley)
    Native American Arts (MFR)

Record/Cassette: Indian Music and Folklore series (BT)

Record: An Anthology of American Indian and Eskimo Music (SSSS)
    As Long as the Grass Shall Grow (SSSS)

Cassettes: Harmony and Discord: The American Indian (SSSS)
    American Indian Medicine (A-T)
    Tribal Myths and Symbols (A-T)
    American Indian Religion (A-T)
    Delawares and Pueblos - A Comparison of Two Indian Cultures (A-T_
    Indian Tribes (CU)
    The Indians Among Us (LL)

Transparencies: Early Indian Tribes (CES)
    American Indians (Hamond, Inc.)

Transparency/Duplicating Book with Filmstrip: North American Indians (SSSS)

Filmstrips (silent): Indian Cultures of the Americas (EBEC; SSSS)
    American Indian Myths (EDC)

Filmstrips (sound): American Indian Legends (EBEC)
    The First Americans: Cultural Patterns (Schloat)
    American Indians (filmstrips one and two in Minorities Have
      Made America Great, Set II) (SSSS)
    The Earth Knowers: The Native Americans Speak (SSSS; MM)
    Indians of the Western Hemisphere (LL)
    Early Indian Cultures of North America (FW)
    Indians of North America (NGS)
    The American Indian: A Dispossessed People (GA)
    We Are Indians: American Indian Literature (GA)

Prints: Indians: The First Americans (Scholastic)
    Famous Indians Posters (PF)
    Gallery of Early Americans (PF)
    Early Indian Cultures of North America (FW)
    The Mankind Portfolio of Six Indian Portraits (Mankind)

<u>Instructional Aids</u>, cont.

Multi-media Kits: <u>Indians of North America</u>   (SSSS)

Simulations: <u>MAHOPA: A Simulation of the History and Culture of the North American Indian</u>   (SSSS)

Activity Boxes: <u>American Indian</u>   (SSSS)

Student and Teacher Resources

Benedict, Ruth
   1961 <u>Patterns of Culture</u> (New York: Houghton-Mifflin Co.)

Brandon, William
   1961 <u>American Heritage Book of Indians</u> (New York: McGraw-Hill Book Co.)

Costo, Rupert
   1974 <u>Contributions and Achievements of the American Indian</u> (San Francisco: Indian Historian Press, Inc.).

Dockstader, Frederick J.
   1966 <u>Indian Art in America: The Arts and Crafts of the North American Indian</u> (Greenwich, Conn.: New York Graphic Society, Ltd.).

Driver, Harold E.
   1964 <u>The Americas on the Eve of Discovery</u> (Englewood Cliffs, NJ: Prentice-Hall Inc.).

   1969 <u>Indians of North America</u> (Chicago, Ill.: University of Chicago Press).

Eggan, Fred <u>et al</u>.
   1955 <u>Social Anthropology of North American Tribes</u> (Chicago, Ill.: University of Chicago Press).

Farb, Peter
   1968 <u>Man's Rise to Civilization as Shown by the Indians of North America from Primeval Times to the Coming of the Industrial State</u> (New York: E.P. Dutton and Co., Inc.).

Gabarino, Merwyn S.
   1976 <u>Native American Heritage</u> (Boston: Little, Brown, and Company)

Henry, Jeannette ed.
   1970 <u>Index to Literature on the American Indian</u> (San Francisco: Indian Historian Press, Inc.).

   1972 <u>The American Indian Reader: Anthropology</u> (San Francisco: Indian Historian Press, Inc.).

Hodge, Frederick W. ed.
   1912 <u>Handbook of American Indians, North of Mexico</u> (Westport, Conn.: Greenwood Press, Inc.).

Josephy, Alvin M., Jr.
    1968 <u>Indian Heritage of America</u> (Westminster, Md.: Alfred A. Knopf, Inc.).

Kroeber, Alfred L.
    1939 <u>Cultural and Natural Areas of Native North America</u> (University of
        California Publications in American Archaeology and Ethnology,vol.38).
Linton, Ralph
    1940 <u>Acculturation in Seven Indian Tribes</u> (Gloucester, Mass.: Peter Smith
        Publisher, Inc,).

Marriott, Alice and Carol K. Rachlin
    1972 <u>American Indian Mythology</u> (New York: Apollo Editions).

Mead, Margaret and Ruth Bunzel, ed.
    1960 <u>The Golden Age of American Anthropology</u> (New York: George Braziller Inc.).

Newcomb, W.W., Jr.
    1974 <u>North American Indians: An Anthropological Perspective</u> (Englewood
        Cliffs, New Jersey: Prentice-Hall, Inc.).

Oswalt, Wendell H.
    1973 <u>This Land Was Theirs: A Study of the North American Indian</u> (New York:
        John Wiley and Son's, Inc.).

Owen, R.C. <u>et al</u>.
    1967 <u>North American Indians: A Sourcebook</u> (New York: Macmillan Publishing
        Co., Inc.).

Silverberg, Robert
    1971 <u>Home of the Red Man</u> (Buffalo, New York: Washington Square Press, Inc.).

Smith, Dwight, ed.
    1974 <u>Indians of the United States and Canada: A Bibliography</u> (Santa Barbara,
        California: American Bibliographic Center-Clio Press).

Spencer, Robert <u>et al</u>.
    1965 <u>Native Americans</u> (Scranton, Penn.: Harper and Row Publishers, Inc.).

Swanton, John
    1968 <u>Indian Tribes of North America</u> (St. Clair Shores, Mich.: Scholarly Press).

Terrell, John Upton
    1974 <u>American Indian Almanac</u> (New York: Apollo Editions).

Underhill, Ruth
    1972 <u>Red Man's Religion: Beliefs and Practices of the Indians North of
        Mexico</u> (Chicago, Ill.: University of Chicago Press).

Vlahos, Olivia
    1971 <u>New World Beginnings: Indian Cultures in the Americas</u> (New York:
        Viking Press, Inc.).

The following periodicals frequently contain articles on American Indian cultures:

<u>American Anthropologist</u>
<u>Current Anthropology</u>

Ethnology
Natural History
Folklore
Ethnohistory
Journal of Anthropological Research
   (formerly Southwestern Journal of Anthropology)
American Ethnologist

<u>Anthropological Terms Used in the Study of American Indian Cultures</u>
  (compiled from Victor Barnouw's AN INTRODUCTION TO ANTHROPOLOGY: ETHNOLOGY and
   Clyde Woods' CULTURE CHANGE)

A <u>CLAN</u> is a unilineal descent group, the members of which believe that they are
re<u>l</u>ated to one another from a common ancestor or ancestress. The same definition
could be given for a lineage, except that in a lineage the members are able to
trace their descent to known forbear; while in a clan the common ancestor is more
distant and usually mythical.

<u>UNILINEAL DESCENT</u> means that kin relationship is traced through one line, either
through males (PATRILINEAL DESCENT) or else through females (MATRILINEAL DESCENT);
in societies having patrilineal descent, property and titles are passed from
father to son; in matrilineal societies they are handed down from a man to his
sister's son.

<u>BILATERAL DESCENT</u>: Equally related to the mother's and father's people

<u>PHRATRY</u>: Two or more clans linked together to form one social unit.

<u>MOIETY</u>: A division of the clan into two groups.

<u>PATRILOCAL RESIDENCE</u>: Custom whereby a bride goes to live with or near her husband's
patrilineal kinsmen.

<u>MATRILOCAL RESIDENCE</u>: Custom whereby the married couple live with or near the
wife's female matrilineal kinsmen.

<u>EXOGAMY</u> is a general term for the requirement to marry outside a particular group.

<u>ENDOGAMY</u> is the requirement to marry within a particular group.

<u>POLYGYMY</u>: A form of marriage involving one man and more than one woman.

<u>POLYANDRY</u>: A form of marriage involving one woman and more than one man.

<u>LEVIRATE</u>: The custom whereby, when a man dies, his widow is expected to marry one
of her dead husband's brothers.

<u>SORORATE</u>: The custom whereby, when a woman dies, her husband is expected to marry
one of his dead wife's sisters.

<u>CULTURE</u>: The way of life of a group of people, the configuration of all of the more
or less stereotyped patterns of learned behavior which are handed down from one
generation to the next through the means of language and imitation.

<u>CULTURE CHANGE</u>: Any modification in the way of life of a people whether consequent
to internal developments or to contact between peoples with unlike ways of life.

<u>ACCULTURATION</u>: Change which occurs when two or more previously autonomous cultural
traditions come into continuous contact with sufficient intensity to promote
extensive changes in one or more areas.

<u>ASSIMILATION</u>: The process whereby two or more previously separate cultural traditions
are combined to produce something new.

Terms, con't.

CULTURAL RELATIVITY: The notion that practices should only be evaluated in terms
of the cultural setting in which they take place.

I.   Subsistence Patterns

      A. Division of Labor

II.   Settlement Patterns

III. Material Culture

      A. Dwellings
      B. Clothing
      C. Household goods

IV.   Political Organization

V.   Social Organization

      A. Kinship and Descent
      B. Form of family
      C. Residence patterns
      D. Voluntary associations

VI.   Religion

      A. Ceremonialism
      B. Religious societies

VII. The Arts

<u>Oral Reports on North American Indian Tribes</u>

Each oral report should be from 5 to 10 minutes in length. The scope of the report should cover 1) distinguishing cultural characteristics, 2) historical role and 3) present situation, i.e., population, location of tribe and other pertinent information. <u>Only one report per tribe</u>.

Suggested Sources: <u>American Indian Almanac</u> by John Terrell
<u>The Native Americans</u> by Spencer and Jenning
<u>Indian Tribes of the United States</u> by John Swanton
<u>Handbook on Indians North of Mexico</u> by Fredrick Hodge

Partial List of Indian Tribes:

I. Tribes of the <u>Northeast</u>   and   <u>Southeast</u>

Abnaki	Cherokee
Pasamaquoddy	Chickasaw
Pennocook	Creek
Penobscot	Choctaw
Wampanoag	Seminole
Narragansett	Yamasee
Pequot	Natchez
Delaware	Calusa
Erie	
Huron	
Ottawa	
Iroquois	
Cayuga	
Mohawk	
Oneida	
Onandaga	
Seneca	
Shawnee	
Sauk	
Fox	
Kickapoo	
Objibwa	

II. Tribes of the <u>Plains</u>   and   <u>Southwest</u>

Blackfoot	Apache
Gros Ventre	Jicarilla
Crow	Mescalero
Assiniboin	Chiricahua
Hidatsa	Navajo
Mandan	Hopi
Sioux	Zuni
Iowa	Pueblo
Ponca	Papago
Pawnee	Pima
Cheyenne	Mohave
Arapaho	Yuma
Kiowa	Havasupai
Osage	
Comanche	
Caddo	

18

III. Tribes of the

Plateau

Flathead
Coeur D'Alene
Spokane
Nez Perce
Yakima
Klamath
Modoc

Great Basin

Shoshone
N. Paiute
S. Paiute
Ute
Washo
Chemhuevi
Serrano
Cahuilla

California

Luiseno
Gabrielino
Chumash
Yokuts
Pomo
Maidu
Yana
Shasta
Salinan

Northwest

Yurok
Tillamook
Quinault
Puyallup
Nisqually

Arctic

Point Barrow Eskimo
Aleut

UNIT TWO

Prehistory of the American Indian

Objectives

At the conclusion of this unit the student will be able to:

Identify and locate major archaeological sites in North America

Compare and contrast various theories regarding origins of the American Indian

Compare and contrast subsistence patterns, technological innovations, social and political organization of the evolutionary cultural stages in prehistoric North America

Outline

I. ORIGINS OF THE AMERICAN INDIAN

   A. Lost Continents Theory
       1. Atlantis
       2. Mu
   B. Descendants of Original Tribes of Israel
       1. Mormon belief
   C. Transpacific (Kon-Tiki) Theory
   D. Bering Strait Land Bridge
   E. Origin Myths of North American Indian Tribes

II. PREHISTORY

   A. Big Game Hunters (Paleo-Indian Period)
       1. Subsistence patterns
       2. Social organization
       3. Major sites/cultural traditions
           a. Clovis
           b. Folsom
           c. Plano
   B. Foragers (Archaic Period)
       1. Subsistence patterns
       2. Social organization
       3. Major sites/cultural traditions
           a. Eastern
           b. Western (Desert)
   C. Later Specializations
       1. Woodland
           a. Adena-Hopewell
           b. Mississippian
       2. Plains
       3. Southwest
           a. Mogollon
           b. Hohokam
           c. Anasazi

Points to Emphasize

American Indian origin myths are comparable to the story of creation, Genesis, in the Christian tradition.

Differences in prehistoric cultural traditions can be explained as specialized adaptations to different environmental conditions.

The Indians were in North America long before Europeans "discovered" America.

Activities

Have students present an origin myth of an American Indian.

Write a narrative on "A Day in the Life of an Paleo-Indian".

Plan a field trip to a nearby museum whose collections contain Indian artifacts. Have students turn in a written report about their visit to the museum or discuss in class.

Instructional Aids

Maps: (1) Migration routes across the Bering Strait and into North and
                South America
            (2) Major archaeological sites and cultural traditions in North America

Films: The First Americans (Berkeley, Minnesota, Illinois, Indiana)
            Prehistoric Men (Xerox)

Filmstrips (sound): How the Indians Discovered a New World (filmstrip number
                     five in Man on the Move: An Introduction to Anthropology)
                     (SSSS; Valiant; CA)

Transparency: Came From Siberia (CES)

Student and Teacher Resources

Brennan, Louis
    1970   American Dawn: A New Model of American Prehistory (New York: Macmillan
            Publishing Co., Inc.)

Ceram, C.W.
    1971   First American: A Story of North American Archaeology (New York: .
            Harcourt, Brace Jovanovich, Inc.).

Claiborne, Robert
    1973   First Americans (Morristown, New Jersey: Silver Burdett Co.).

Student and Teacher Resources, con't.

Coy, Harold
    1973   Man Comes to America (Waltham, Mass.: Little, Brown and Co.).

Fitting, James ed.
    1973   The Development of North American Archaeology (Garden City, New York:
            Doubleday and Co., Inc.).

Goldstein, Shirley ed.
    1975   North America (New York: St. Martin's Press, Inc.).

Hester, Joseph A. and Keith MacGawan
    1962   Early Man in the New World (Garden City, New York: Natural
            History Press).

*Huddleston, Lee E.
    1967   Origins of the American Indians: European Concepts (Austin, Texas:
            University of Texas Press).

*Jennings, Jesse D. and Edward Norbeck eds.
    1964   Prehistoric Man in the New World (Chicago, Ill.: University of
            Chicago Press).

*   1974   Prehistory of North America (New York: McGraw-Hill Book Co.).

*Kidder, Alfred
    1962   Introduction to the Study of Southwest Archaeology (New Haven, Conn.:
            Yale University Press).

McKern, Sharon S.
    1972   Exploring the Unknown: Mysteries in American Archaeology (New
            York: Praeger Publications).

*MacNeish, Richard S. et al.
    1973   Early Man in America: Readings from Scientific American (San Francisco:
            W.H. Freeman and Co.).

Patterson, Thomas C.
    1973   America's Past: A New World Archaeology (Glenview, Ill.: Scott
            Foresman and Co.).

Sanders, William and Joseph P. Marino
    1970   New World Prehistory (Englewood Cliffs, New Jersey: Prentice-Hall, Inc.).

Stewart, T.D.
    1973   The People of America (New York: Charles Scribner's Sons).

Wauchope, Robert
    1962   Lost Tribes and Sunken Continents: Myth Method in the Study of
            American Indians (Chicago, Ill.: University of Chicago Press).

*Wedel, Waldo R.
            Prehistoric Man on the Great Plains (Norman: University of Oklahoma Press).

Student and Teacher Resources, con't.

*Willey, Gordon
    1966   Introduction to American Archaeology: North and Middle America
           (Englewood Cliffs, New Jersey: Prentice-Hall, Inc.).

The following periodicals frequently contain articles on American Indian prehistory
(North American archaeology):

    American Antiquity
    Archaeology
    American Journal of Physical Anthropology
    Scientific American
    Arctic Anthropology
    Archaeology of Eastern North America
    Pennsylvania Archaeologist

UNIT THREE

American Indian Cultures, East of the Mississippi

Objectives

At the end of this unit, the student will be able to:

Identify[1]:

Algonquians	"Hodenosaunee"	Pine Tree Chiefs
Beloved Men	"Honored Men"	Powhatan Confederacy
calumet	Hot house	"puskita"
Council of Fifty	Huron Confederacy	Red Clans
Deganawidah	longhouse	sachem
Dream Festival	Manitou	"Stinkards"
False Face Society	Miami Confederacy	"Suns"
Grand Medicine Society	Miko	Tuscaroras
Great Sun	Muskhogen	wampum
Green Corn Ceremony	"Nobles"	White Clans
Hiawatha	orenda	wigwam

Compare and contrast selected tribes for the Northeast and Southeast in the following areas: (1) material culture; (2) subsistence patterns; (3) political organization; (4) social organization; and (5) religion

Identify and locate major tribes in the Northeast and Southeast

Compare the structure and division of powers of the federal government with the Iroquois Confederacy

Compare and contrast the stereotyped image of the Indian with Indians of the Northeast and Southeast

Outline

I. INDIAN CULTURES, EAST OF THE MISSISSIPPI

    A.   Indians of the Northeast
        1. Survey of Indian tribes in northeastern U.S.
        2. General characteristics of tribes within culture area (see Kroeber, 1939).
        3. Case Studies: Iroquois, Eastern Algonquians: Penobscot; Eastern Sub-Arctic: Objibwa[2]
            a. Subsistence patterns
            b. Political organization
            c. Social organization
            d. Material culture
            e. Religion

    B.   Indians of the Southeast
        1. Survey of Indian tribes in southeastern U.S.
        2. General characteristics of tribes within culture area (see

Outline, con't.

                Kroeber, 1939)
        3. Case studies: Natchez, Creeks[3]
           a. Subsistence patterns
           b. Material culture
           c. Social organization
           d. Political organization
           e. Religion

Points to Emphasize

The sophisticated and fluid political structure of the Iroquois and Creek Confederacies

Comparison of the political organization of the Iroquois and the Eastern Algonquians

The importance of the role of women in agriculturally-based Indian societies especially the Iroquois and Natchez

Activities

Map Assignment: Locate given Indian tribes of the Northeast and Southeast at the time of European contact

Using the above map compare the position of the tribes, east of the Mississippi, at the time of European contact with their present locations. What conclusions can be drawn?

Oral reports on various tribes in the Northeast and Southeast

Instructional Aids

Films: Seminole Indians (Minnesota)
           Longhouse People (Indiana)

Filmstrips (silent):   Indians of the Northeast (EBEC)
                      Indians of the Southeast (EBEC)
                      American Indian Cultures-Plains and Woodland (EBEC)

Transparency: Eastern Indians (Valiant)

Student and Teacher Resources

Axtell, James ed.
    1973   Native American People of the East (New Haven, Conn.: Pendulum Press, Inc.).

Student and Teacher Resources, con't.

Burt, Jesse and Robert B. Ferguson
    1973   Indians of the Southeast: Then and Now (Nashville, Tenn.: Abingdon
            Press).

*Fenton, William N. ed.
    1951   Symposium on Local Diversity in Iroquois Culture (St. Clair Shores,
            Mich.: Scholarly Press).

*Fenton, William N. and John GuLick eds.
    1961   Symposium on Cherokee and Iroquois Culture (St. Clair Shores, Mich.:
            Scholarly Press).

Garbarino, Merwyn S.
    1972   Big Cypress: A Changing Seminole Community (New York: Holt, Rinehart,
            and Winston, Inc.)

Hertzberg, Hazel W.
    1966   The Great Tree and The Long House (New York: Macmillan Publishing
            Co., Inc.).

Johnson, F. Roy
    1972   The Algonquians: Indians of That Part of the New World First Visited
            by the English: Prehistory and Culture (Murfreesboro, NC: Johnson
            Publishing Co.).

Kinietz, W. Vernon
    1965   Indians of the Western Great Lakes, 1615-1760 (Ann Arbor, Mich.:
            University of Michigan Press).

Kraft, Herbert ed.
    1974   A Delaware Indian Symposium (Harrisburg: The Pennsylvania Historical
            and Museum Commission).

Landes, Ruth
    1968   Mystic Lake Sioux: Sociology of the Mdewakantonwan Santee (Madison,
            Wis.: University of Wisconson Press).

Mahon, John K.
    1974   Indians of the Lower South (Pensacola, Fla.: University of West Florida).

Morgan, Lewis Henry
    1972   League of the Iroquois (Secaucus, NJ: Citadel Press).

Quimby, George I.
    1960   Indian Life on the Upper Great Lakes: 11,000 B.C. to A.D. 800
            (Chicago, Ill.: University of Chicago Press).

Ritzenthaler, Robert and Pat Ritzenthaler
    1970   Woodland Indians of the Western Great Lakes (Garden City, New York:
            Natural History Press).

Spindler, George and Louise Spindler
    1971   Dreamers Without Powers: The Menomini Indians (New York: Holt, Rinehart
            and Winston, Inc.).

*Swanton, John
    1943   The Indians of the Southeastern United States (St. Clair Shores, Mich.:
            Scholarly Press).

*   1970   Indian Tribes of the Lower Mississippi Valley and Adjacent Coast of
            the Gulf of Mexico (New York: Johnson Reprint, Corp.).

*Tooker, Elizabeth
    1964   An Ethnography of the Huron Indians, 1615-1649 (St. Clair Shores, Mich.:
            Scholarly Press).

*Wissler, Clark ed.
    1909   The Indians of Greater New York and the Lower Hudson (New York: AMS
            Press, Inc.).

The following periodicals frequently contain articles on American Indian cultures, east of the Mississippi:

    Florida Anthropologist
    Man in the Northeast

[1]These will differ according to the sources used and tribes covered in class. Spencer and Jennings (1965) and Silverberg (1971) provided the basis of the names and terms used here.

[2]The tribes used for case studies will differ according to textbook and instructor's preference. Spencer and Jennings (1965) provide case studies for those listed.

[3]Ibid.

UNIT FOUR
Indian Cultures, West of the Mississippi[1]

Objectives

At the conclusion of this unit, the student will be able to:

Identify:[2]

Basketmaker Culture	kivas
Blessing Way	Okipa ceremony
"Buffalo Bulls"	"Old Settlers"
coup	"outfit"
Dakota Confederation	plank houses
Give Away Feast	potlatch
hogan	Pueblos
Hohokam	Sun Dance
"horse-and-buffalo" complex	tipi
katchinas	totem pole
Kit-foxes	

Describe the role of the horse and buffalo in Plains culture

Compare and contrast selected tribes for the Indian cultures, west of the Mississippi in the following areas: (1) material culture; (2) subsistence patterns; (3) political organization; (4) social organization; and (5) religion

Identify and locate major tribes in the area west of the Mississippi

Outline

I.   TRIBES OF THE GREAT PLAINS[3]

   A.   Survey of tribes, languages and environment
   B.   Case Studies: Mandan, Teton Dakota and Kiowa
       1.   Material culture
       2.   Subsistence patterns
       3.   Political organization
       4.   Social organization
       5.   Religion

II. TRIBES OF THE GREATER SOUTHWEST[4]

   A.   Survey of tribes, languages and environment
   B.   Case Studies: Zuni, Navajo
       1.   Material culture
       2.   Subsistence patterns
       3.   Political organization
       4.   Social organization
       5.   Religion

III. TRIBES OF WESTERN NORTH AMERICA-PLATEAU, GREAT BASIN AND CALIFORNIA[5]

Outline, con't.

    A.   Survey of tribes, environments and language groups
    B.   Case Studies: (use areas listed under I.B for studying the following tribes)
        1. Plateau
            a. Klamath
        2. California
            a. Hupa
            b. Pomo
            c. Luiseno
            d. Mojave
        3. Great Basin
            a. Shoshone

IV. INDIANS OF THE NORTHWEST COAST[6]

    A.   Survey of tribes, language groups, environment
    B.   Case Studies: Kwakiutl and Tlingit
        1. Material culture
        2. Subsistence patterns
        3. Political organization
        4. Social organization
        5. Religion

Points to Emphasize

Plains Indian culture, based on the horse-and-buffalo complex, was a relatively recent phenomenon. It probably did not fully develop until well into the 1700's.

Activities

Map: Locate given Indian tribes, west of the Mississippi at the time of European contact

Oral reports on tribes in California, Pacific Northwest, Great Basin, Plateau, Greater Southwest, and Plains

Instructional Aids

Films: This Was the Time (potlatch) (Berkeley)
           People of the Buffalo (Berkeley, Indiana)
           Indians of California (Berkeley, Indiana)
           Ishi in Two Worlds (Berkeley, Minnesota, Oregon)
           Acorns: Staple Food of California Indians (Berkeley)
           Washoe (Minnesota, Indiana)
           Indians of the Plains-Sun Dance Ceremony (Minnesota, Oregon)
           Way of the Navajo (Minnesota)
           The Navajos-Children of the Gods (Disney, Minnesota)
           Indians of the Southwest (Mac)
           Navajo (Mac)

<u>Instructional Aids</u>, con't.

       <u>The Crooked Beak of Heaven</u> (potlatch) (Time-Life)

Film Loops: <u>Southwest Indians</u> (P-H)
            <u>Plains Indians</u> (P-H)
            <u>Pacific Coast Indians</u> (P-H)

Discovery Packet: <u>Indians of the Southwest</u> (MM)

Cassette: <u>The Hopi Speaks: Message to the World</u> (LL)

Filmstrips (silent):   <u>American Indian Cultures-Plains and Woodland</u> (EBEC)
                     <u>Indians of the Southwest</u> (EBEC)
                     <u>Indians of the Plains</u> (EBEC)
                     <u>Indians and Eskimos of the Northwest</u> (EBEC)

Filmstrips (sound):   <u>The Early Indian Culture in the Southwest</u> (SSSS)
                     <u>Indian Life in North America</u> (Pueblo and Havasupai)(SSSS;EDC)
                     <u>Indians of the Pacific Northwest</u> (EMI)
                     <u>The Pueblo Story</u> (RMI)
                     <u>Southwest Indian Crafts</u> (RMI)
                     <u>The Navajo Story</u> (RMI)
                     <u>Navajo Wildlands</u> (PF)

Simulation: Potlatch (SSSS)

Transparencies: <u>Western Indians</u> (Valiant)
                <u>Hunting Buffalo</u> (CES)

<u>Student and Teacher Resources</u>

Baldwin, Gordon C.
    1973 <u>Indians of the Southwest</u> (New York: G.P. Putnam's Sons).

Basso, Keith H.
    1970 <u>Cibecue Apache</u> (New York: Holt, Rinehart, and Winston, Inc.)

*   1971 <u>Apachean Culture, History and Ethnology</u> (Tuscon: University of Arizona
       Press).

Bean, Lowell
    1972 <u>Mukat's People: The Cahuilla Indians of Southern California</u> (Berkeley:
       University of California Press)

Brown, Vinson
    1969 <u>Pomo Indians of California and Their Neighbors</u> (Healdsburg, Calif.:
       Naturegraph Publishers).

Brusa, Betty W.
    1973 <u>Salinan Indians and Their Neighbors</u> (Healdsburg, Calif.: Naturegraph
       Publishers).

Student and Teacher Resources, con't.

Catlin, George
    1973   Letters and Notes on the Manners, Customs, and Conditions of the
            North American Indians (New York: Dover Publications, Inc.).

*Codere, Helen
    1950   Fighting With Property: A Study of Kwakiutl Potlatching and Warfare
            (Seattle: University of Washington Press).

*D'Azeredo, Warren ed.
    1973   The Washo Indians of California and Nevada (Salt Lake City: University
            of Utah Press).

Downs, James F.
    1966   Two Worlds of the Washo: An Indian Tribe of California and Nevada
            (New York: Holt, Rinehart and Winston, Inc.).

    1972   The Navajo (New York: Holt, Rinehart, and Winston, Inc.).

Dozier, Edward P.
    1965   Hano: A Tewa Indian Community in Arizona (New York: Holt, Rinehart,
            and Winston, Inc.).

    1970   The Pueblo Indians of North America (New York: Holt, Rinehart, and
            Winston, Inc.).

Drucker, Philip
    1963   Indians of the Northwest Coast (Garden City, New York: Natural History
            Press).

*Drucker, Philip and Robert Heizer
    1967   To Make My Name Good: A Re-Examination of the Southern Kwakiutl
            Potlatch (Berkeley: University of California Press).

Dutton, Bertha
    1974   Indians of the American Southwest (Los Angeles: Spectrum Productions).

Erdoes, Richard
    1972   The Sun Dance People: The Plains Indians, Their Past and Present
            (Westminster, Md.: Alfred A. Knopf, Inc.).

*Ewers, John
    1955   The Horse in Blackfoot Indian Culture with Comparative Material from
            Other Western Tribes (St. Clair Shores, Mich.: Scholarly Press).

*   1969   Horse in Blackfoot Indian Culture (New York: Smithsonian Institution
            Press).

Forbes, Jack
    1965   Native Americans of California and Nevada (Healdsburg, Calif.:
            Naturegraph Publishers).

Grinell, George
    1972   Cheyenne Indians, Their History and Ways of Life (Lincoln: University
            of Nebraska Press).

Student and Teacher Resources, con't.

Gunther, Erna
　　1972　Indian Life on the Northwest Coast of North America as Seen by the
　　　　　Early Explorers and Fur Traders During the Last Decades of the
　　　　　18th Century (Chicago: The University of Chicago Press).

Haines, Francis
　　1970　Indians of the Great Basin and Plateau (New York: G.P. Putnam's Sons).

Hayes, H.R.
　　1975　Children of the Raven: The Seven Indian Nations of the Northwest Coast
　　　　　(New York: McGraw-Hill Book Company).

*Hedrick, Basil ed.
　　1973　The Classic Southwest: Readings in Archaeology, Ethnohistory, and
　　　　　Ethnology (De Kalb, Ill.: Northern Illinois University Press).

*Heizer, Robert F. and M.A. Whipple
　　1971　The California Indians: A Source Book (Berkeley: University of
　　　　　California Press).

Hoebel, Edward A.
　　1960　Cheyennes: Indians of the Great Plains (New York: Holt, Rinehart, and
　　　　　Winston, Inc.).

Holder, Preston
　　1974　The Hoe and the Horse on the Plains: A Study of Cultural Development
　　　　　Among North American Indians (Lincoln: University of Nebraska Press).

Hooper, Lucille
　　1972　The Cahuilla Indians (Ramona, Calif.: Fallena Press).

Jorgensen, Joseph
　　1974　The Sun Dance People: Power for the Powerless (Chicago: University of
　　　　　Chicago Press).

Kluckhohn, Clyde and Dorothea Leighton
　　1973　The Navajo (Cambridge, Mass.: Harvard University Press).

*Kroeber, Alfred A.
　　1925　Handbook of the Indians of California (Berkeley: California Book Co.).

*Lewis, Oscar
　　1942　Effects of White Contact Upon Blackfoot Culture, with Special Reference
　　　　　to the Role of the Fur Trader (Seattle: University of Washington Press).

Lowie, Robert H.
　　1956　Crow Indians (New York: Holt, Rinehart, and Winston, Inc.).

　　1963　Indians of the Plains (Garden City, New York: Natural History Press).

McFeat, Tom ed.
　　1967　Indians of the North Pacific Coast (Seattle: University of Washington
　　　　　Press).

Student and Teacher Resources, con't.

McFee, Malcolm
    1972   Modern Blackfeet: Montanans on a Reservation (New York: Holt, Rinehart, and Winston, Inc.).

Mails, Thomas E.
    1973   Dog Soldiers, Bear Men and Buffalo Women: The Societies and Cults of the Plains Indians (Englewood Cliffs, NJ: Prentice-Hall, Inc.).

    1972   Mystic Warriors of the Plains (Garden City, New York: Doubleday).

Marriott, Alice
    1968   Kiowa Years (New York: Macmillan Publishing Co., Inc.).

Metcalf, P. Richard
    1973   The Native American People of the West (West Haven, Conn.: Pendulum Press).

*Mishkin, Bernard
    1940   Rank and Warfare Among the Plains Indians (Seattle: University of Washington Press).

Newcomb, W.W., Jr.
    1961   Indians of Texas: From Prehistoric to Modern Times (Austin: University of Texas Press).

Oosterman, Gordon
    1973   The People: Three Indian Tribes of the Southwest (Grand Rapids, Mich.: William B. Eerdmans Publishing Co.).

Opler, Morris
    1969   Apache Odyssey (New York: Holt, Rinehart, and Winston, Inc.).

Ortiz, Alfonso
    1969   Tewa World: Space, Time, and Being in a Pueblo Society (Chicago: University of Chicago Press).

Powers, William K.
    1969   Indians of the Northern Plains (New York: G.P. Putnam's Sons).

    1972   Indians of the Southern Plains (New York: G.P. Putnam's Sons).

Roe, Frank
    1955   The Indian and the Horse (Norman: University of Oklahoma Press).

Steward, Julian H.
    1970   Basin-Plateau Aboriginal Sociopolitical Groups (Salt Lake City: University of Utah Press).

Terrell, John Upton
    1972   The Navajos: The Past and Present of a Great People (Scranton, Penn.: Harper and Row Publishers, Inc.).

<u>Student and Teacher Resources</u>, con't.

The following periodicals frequently contain articles on American Indian cultures, west of the Mississippi:

<u>Plains Anthropologist</u>
<u>Northwest Anthropological Notes</u>
<u>Masterkey</u>
<u>Journal of California Anthropology</u>

FOOTNOTES

[1]This unit may be broken down into the following culture areas: Greater Southwest; Pacific Northwest; California; Plains and Prairies; and Great Basin/ Plateau

[2]These will differ to the sources used and tribes covered in class. Spencer and Jennings (1965) and Silverberg (1971) provided the basis of the names and terms used here.

[3]Spencer and Jennings (1965) provides material for the case studies listed.

[4]Ibid.

[5]Ibid.

[6]Ibid.

INTRODUCTION TO UNITS ON AMERICAN INDIAN HISTORY

Objectives

At the conclusion of the teaching units on American Indian history, the student will be able to:

Identify influential Indian leaders, past and present

Outline major phases in American Indian history

Compare and contrast selected revitalization movements in North America

Describe major government policies toward the American Indian

Evaluate important court cases concerning the legal status of Indians and Indian tribes

Criticize the stereotyped role of the Indian in American history

Describe intertribal relations among North American Indians

Evaluate the effects of white contact on intertribal relations

Evaluate the role of the Indian in American history

Criticize the effects of government policy on intratribal relations

Outline

I.   SURVEY OF MAJOR PHASES IN AMERICAN INDIAN HISTORY[1]

    A.   Many Nations, 1540-1794
    B.   New Orientations, 1763-1848
    C.   Dependent Domestic Nations, 1831-1898
    D.   The Colonial Pattern, 1871-1934
    E.   American Citizens, 1924-1967

Points to Emphasize

Since the Indians were in North America first, the Europeans were the intruders.

Indian lands (Reservations) were not given to them but are the remnants of their aboriginal lands.

Methods in government policies have changed but not the basic goal: assimilation of the Indian in American society. For this reason, government programs are destined to fail unless the overall objective is changed.

Activities

Oral or written reports on selected articles or topics on American Indian history (see pages 44- 45 for suggested format).

Instructional Aids

Films: The Indians (Xerox)
         Home of the Brave (Pyramid)

Filmstrips (sound): Legal and Illegal: The Dispossession of the Indians (SSSS; MM)
                    Indians (SSSS; MM)
                    The American Indian: A Study in Depth (SSSS, Schloat)

Posters: A Portfolio of Outstanding Contemporary American Indians (SSSS)
          Historical American Indian Biographies (SSSS)
          Contemporary American Indian Biographies (SSSS)
          Famous Indian Posters (PF)
          Gallery of Early Americans (PF)

Record: As Long as the Grass Shall Grow (SSSS)

Prints: Indians: The First Americans (Scholastic)

Cassette: Famous American Indian Leaders (CU)

Map: Indian Land Cessions (AAG)
      Indian Land Areas (BIA)

Simulation: Indians View Americans, Americans View Indians (Divided into three
            sections: Red Men and White Men; The Black Hawk War and Cherokee
            Removal; The Sun Dance and Ghost Dance) (EAV)

Cassettes: Folklore vs. Reality-Three Views of the Indian in American History (A-T)
            Genocide: American Style (A-T)
            History of the Forked Tongue (Parts I and II) (A-T)
            Harmony and Discord: The American Indian (SSSS)

Jackdaw Kit: Indian Resistance (SSSS)

Student and Teacher Resources

Andrews, Ralph
     1971   Indian Leaders Who Helped Shape America (Seattle: Superior Publishing
            Co.).

Armstrong, Virginia ed.
     1972   I Have Spoken: American History Through the Voices of the Indians
            (New York: Pocket Books, Inc.).

Student and Teacher Resources, con't.

*Berkhofer, Robert F., Jr.
    1972   Salvation and the Savage: An Analysis of Protestant Missions and
            American Indian Response, 1787-1862 (New York: Atheneum Publishers).

Billington, Ray Allen
    1974   Westward Expansion (New York: Macmillan Publishing Company, Inc.).

Britt, Albert
    1938   Great Indian Chiefs (Plainview, New York: Books for Libraries, Inc.).

Capps, Ben
    1973   The Indians (Morristown, NJ: Silver Burdett Co.).

Chamberlin, J.
    1975   The Harrowing of Eden: White Attitudes Toward Native Americans (New
            York: Seabury Press, Inc.).

*Cohen, Felix
    1942   Handbook of Federal Indian Law (Albuquerque: University of New
            Mexico Press).

Council on Interracial Books for Children ed.
    1971   Chronicles of American Indian Protest (New York: Fawcett World Library).

David, Jay ed.
    1972   The American Indian: The First Victim (New York: William Morrow
            and Co., Inc.).

Debo, Angie
    1970   A History of the Indians of the United States (Norman: University of
            Oklahoma Press).

DeLoria, Vine, Jr.
    1971   Of Utmost Good Faith (New York: Bantam Books).

Dennis, Henry C.
    1971   American Indian, 1492-1970: A Chronology and Fact Book (Dobbs Ferry,
            New York: Oceana Publications).

Ellis, Richard N. ed.
    1972   Western American Indian: Case Studies in Tribal History (Lincoln:
            University of Nebraska Press).

Fey, Harold E. and D'Arcy McNickle
    1970   Indians and Other Americans: Two Ways of Life Meet (Scranton, Penn.:
            Harper and Row Publishers, Inc.).

Forbes, Jack
    1964   Indians in America's Past (Englewood Cliffs, NJ: Prentice-Hall, Inc.).

Georgakas, Dan
    1973   The Broken Hoop: A History of Native Americans from the Atlantic Coast
            to the Plains (Garden City, New York: Doubleday and Co., Inc.).

Student and Teacher Resources, con't.

Georgakas, Dan, con't.
    1973   Red Shadows: A History of Native Americans from the Desert to the
            Pacific Coast (Garden City, New York: Doubleday and Co,m Inc.).

Gibson, Michael
    1974   The American Indian: From Colonial Times to the Present (New York:
            G.P. Putnam's Sons).

Gibson, Arrell
    1976   The West in the Life of the Nation (Lexington, Mass.: D.C. Heath and Co.).

Hagan, William
    1961   American Indians (Chicago: University of Chicago Press).

Hamilton, Charles ed.
    1972   Cry of the Thunderbird: The American Indian's Own Story (Norman:
            University of Oklahoma Press).

Heard, J. Norman
    1973   White into Red: A Study of the Assimilation of White Persons Captured
            by Indians (Metuchen, NJ: Scarecrow Press, Inc.).

Henry, Jeannette ed.
    1970-   Index to the Literature on the American Indian (San Francisco: Indian
            Historian Press, Inc.).

    1974   American Indian Reader: History (San Francisco: Indian Historian
            Press, Inc.).

Hodge, Frederick W. ed.
    1912   Handbook of American Indians, North of Mexico (Westport, Conn.:
            Greenwood Press, Inc.).

Holmes, Vera
    1950   History of the Americas: From Discovery to Nationhood (New York:
            Ronald Press Co.).

Hudson, Charles ed.
    1975   Four Centuries of Southern Indians (Athens: University of Georgia Press).

Hundley, Norris. ed.
    1974   The American Indian (Santa Barbara, CA: American Bibliographic Center-
            Clio Press).

Jones, Charles, ed.
    1972   Look to the Mountain Top (San Jose, CA: H.M. Gousha).

Josephy, Alvin ., Jr.
    1961   Patriot Chiefs: A Chronicle of American Indian Resistence (New York:
            Viking Press, Inc.).

    1971   Indian Resistance: The Patriot Chiefs (Jackdaw) (New York: Grossman
            Publishers, Inc.).

*Kappler, Charles J. comp.
    1972   Indian Treaties, 1778-1883 (New York: Interland Publishing, Inc.).

Student and Teacher Resources, con't.

Leacock, Eleanor and Nancy O. Lurie
   1971   North American Indians in Historical Perspective (Westminister, MD: Random House, Inc.).

McNickle, D'Arcy
   1966   The Indian Tribes of the United States: Ethnic and Cultural Survival (New York: Oxford University Press).

   1972   They Came Here First: The Epic of the American Indian (New York: Octagon Books).

   1973   Native American Tribalism (New York: Oxford University Press).

*Macleod, William Christie
   1928   The American Indian Frontier (New York: Alfred A. Knopf, Inc.).

Marriott, Alive and Carol K. Rachlin
   1969   American Epic: The Story of the American Indian (New York: G.P. Putnam's Sons).

Meyer, William
   1971   Native Americans: The New Indian Resistance (New York: International Publishers Co., Inc.).

Mosquin, Wayne and Charles Van Doren, eds.
   1974   This Country Was Ours: A Documentary History of the American Indian (New York: Praeger Publishers).

Myers, J. Jay
   1972   Red Chiefs and White Challengers (Buffalo, New York: Washington Square Press, Inc.).

Nichols, Roger L. and George Adams eds.
   1971   American Indians: Past and Present (Lexington, Mass.: Xerox College Publishing).

Pearce, Roy H. and J.H. Miller
   1965   Savages of America: A Study of the Indian and the Idea of Civilization (Baltimore, MD: John Hopkin's Press).

Pearson, Keith L.
   1973   The Indian in American History (New York: Harcourt, Brace, and Jovanovich, Inc.).

Peithmann, Irvin M.
   1964   Broken Peace Pipes: A Four Hundred Year History of the American Indian (Springfield, Ill.: Charles C. Thomas Publishers).

*Price, Monroe
   1973   Law and the American Indian (Indianapolis: Bobbs-Merrill Co., Inc.).

Prucha, Francis and William Hagan, Alvin M. Josephy, Jr.
   1971   American Indian Policy (Indianapolis: Indiana Historical Society).

Prucha, Francis P. ed.
    1975   Documents of U.S. Indian Policy (Lincoln: University of Nebraska Press).

    1971   Indian in American History (New York: Holt, Rinehart, and Winston, Inc.).

Roe, Melvin ed
    1971   Readings in the History of the American Indian (New York: Mss Information Corp.).

*Royce, Charles C.
    1971   Indian Land Cessions in the United States (New York: Arnold Press).

Sanders, Thomas and Walter W. Peck eds.
    1973   Literature of the American Indian (Riverside, NJ: Glencoe Press).

Schmeckebier, Laurence F.
    1927   The Office of Indian Affairs, Its History, Activities, and Organizations (New York: AMS Press, Inc.).

Slotkin, Richard
    1973   Regeneration Through Violence: The Mythology of the American Frontier, 1600-1860 (Middletown, Conn.: Wesleyan University).

Spicer, Edward H.
    1969   A Short History of the Indians of the United States (Cincinnati, Ohio: Van Nostrand Reinhold Co.).

Sutton, Irme
    1975   Indian LandTennure: Bibliographical Essay and a Guide to the Literature (New York: Clearwater Publishing Co.).

Svensson, Frances
    1973   The Ethnics in American Politics: American Indians (Long Island City, New York: Burgess Publishing Co.).

Tebbel, John
    1966   The Compact History of Indian Wars (New York: Tower Publications, Inc.).

Tyler, S. Lyman
    1973   A History of Indian Policy (Washington, D.C.: Government Printing Office).

Underhill, Ruth
    1971   Red Man's America: A History of the Indians of the United States (Chicago: University of Chicago Press).

U.S. Department of Commerce
    1974   Federal and State Indian Reservations and Indian Trust Areas (Washington, D.C.: U.S. Government Printing Office).

Van DerBeets, Richard ed.
    1973   Held Captive by Indians: Selected Narratives, 1642-1836 (Knoxville, Tenn.: University of Tennessee Press).

Student and Teacher Resources, con't.

Vanderwerth, W.C.
1971   Indian Oratory: A Collection of Famous Speeches by Noted Indian Chieftains (Norman: University of Oklahoma Press).

Vogel, Virgil V.
1968   Indian in American History (Evanston, Ill.: Integrated Education Associates).

1972   This Country Was Ours: A Documentary History of the American Indian (Scranton, Penn.: Harper and Row Publishers, Inc.).

Washburn, Wilcomb E.
1964   Indian and the White Man (Garden City, New York: Doubleday and Co, Inc.).

1971   Red Man's Land-White Man's Law (New York: Charles Scribner's Sons).

1973   American Indians and the United States (New York: Random House, Inc.).

1975   The Indian in America (Scranton, Penn.: Harper and Row Publishers, Inc.).

Wax, Murray L.
1971   Indian-Americans: Unity and Diversity (Englewood Cliffs, NJ: Prentice-Hall, Inc.).

Wax, Murray L. and Robert Buchanan eds.
1975   Solving "the Indian Problem": The White Man's Burdensome Business (New York: Franklin Watts, Inc.).

Wise, Jennings and Vine Deloria, Jr.
1971   Red Man in the New World Drama (New York: Macmillan Publishing Co, Inc.).

Wissler, Clark
1966   Indians of the United States: Four Centuries of Their History and Culture (Garden City, New York: Doubleday and Co., Inc.).

Worchester, Donald E., ed.
1975   Forked Tongues and Broken Treaties (Caldwell, Idaho: The Caxton Printers, Ltd.).

Worton, Stanley
1974   The First Americans (Rochelle Park, NJ: Hayden Book Co., Inc.).

Wrone, David R. and Russell Nelson, Jr. eds.
1973   Who's the Savage: A Documentary History of the Mistreatment of the Native North Americans (Greenwich, Conn.: Fawcett Publications).

The following periodicals frequently contain articles on American Indian history:

American Heritage
American History Illustrated
Indian Historian
Proceedings of the American
    Philosophical Society

Journal of American History (formerly Mississippi Valley Historical Rev.)
Journal of Ethnic Studies
Pacific Historical Review
American Indian Quarterly

Also see titles published in The Civilization of the American Indian Series by the University of Oklahoma Press.

FORMAT FOR ORAL REPORTS
ON SELECTED READINGS IN AMERICAN INDIAN HISTORY

Your presentation should be divided into two parts: The first part should summarize the main points of the article. The second half should attempt to analyze the article in light of assigned readings in class and lecture material. The analysis includes your opinion of the article, its strengths and its weaknesses.

All books and articles are on reserve in the S.B.V.C. library.

A. The Patriot Chiefs by Alvin Josephy, Jr.

B. Attitudes of Colonial Powers toward the American Indian edited by Howard Peckham

C. Great Indian Chiefs by Albert Britt

D. Expansion and American Indian Policy, 1783-1812 by R. Horsman

E. A Short History of the Indians of the United States by Edward Spicer

F. Red Chiefs and White Challengers by J. Jay Myers

G. Red Man's Reservations by Clark Wissler

H. Indians and Other Americans by Harold Fey and D'Arcy McNickle

I. Indians of the Americas by John Collier

J. Custer Died For Your Sins by Vine DeLoria, Jr.

K. Native Americans Today: Sociological Perspectives by Bahr, Chadwick, and Day

L. Seventeenth Century America: Essays in Colonial History edited by James Smith

M. Cycles of Conquest by Edward Spicer

N. Bury My Heart at Wounded Knee by Dee Brown

Early Relations

(1) "The Betrayal of King Philip" in (A)
(2) "Pope and the Great Pueblo Uprising" in (A)
(3) "Indian Cultural Adjustment to European Civilization" by Nancy Lurie in (L)
(4) "The Wilderness War of Pontiac" in (A)
(5) Joseph Brant in (C)
(6) "The Moral and Legal Justification for Dispossessing the Indian" by Washburn in (L)
(7) "The French and the Indians" by Mason Wade in (B)
(8) "British-Colonial Attitudes and Policies toward the Indian in American Colonies" by Wilbur Jacobs in (B)
(9) "The Spanish Program" in (M)

Formation of Federal Policy

(10) "Aims of the New Government" in (D)
(11) "The Handsome Lake Religion" and "The Algonkian Prophets" in (E)

Indian Removal

(12) "John Ross" in (F)

(13) "Alternatives to Indian Removal Before 1838" by Sharon Lindley, Stanford Quarterly Review

(14) "Indian Allotment Removal and Land Allotment: The Civilized Tribes and Jacksonian Justice" by Mary Young, Mississippi Historical Review

Conquest and Confinement: California and the Northwest

(15) "Native American Experience in California" by Jack Forbes, Southern California Quarterly and "Atomization of the California Indians" in (E)

(16) Chief Joseph in (A)

(17) "Ordeal of Captain Jack" in (N)

Conquest and Confinement: The Plains

(18) "Chochise" in (F)

(19) "Sitting Bull" in (F)

(20) "Cheyenne Exodus" in (N)

Reservation Life

(21) "Ration Tickets and Beef Issue" and "The Great Depression in Indian Country" in (G)

(22) "New Messiahs" and "The Decline of Local Government" in (E)

(23) "Wounded Knee" in (N)

FOOTNOTES

[1]Structured after Spicer, 1969.

UNIT FIVE
Early Relations-Indians and Europeans

Objectives

At the end of this unit, the student will be able to:

Summarize Indian relations with major European expeditions into North America

Appraise the effects that the treatment received from the early explorers had on the Indian's perception fo the white man

Compare and contrast the early expeditions of the Spanish, French, and English in the area of Indian relations

Describe Indian response to the early European expeditions

Outline

I.   INDIAN RESPONSE TO MAJOR EXPEDITIONS INTO NORTH AMERICA
     A.   Indian response to expeditions in the Northeast and Southeast
          1.   Jean Ribaut
          2.   Sir Walter Raleigh
          3.   Champlain
          4.   Cabeza de Vaca
          5.   Hernando DeSoto
          6.   Etienne Brule
          7.   Jean Nicolet
          8.   Henry Hudson
     B.   Indian response to expeditions in the Southwest
          1.   Coronado
          2.   Onate
     C.   Indian response to expeditions on the Pacific Coast
          1.   Drake
          2.   Cabrillo

Points to Emphasize

When Columbus "discovered" America there were already approximately one million Indians living on the North American continent alone (not counting the seven million in Middle and South America).

The only hostility encountered from Indians were in those areas where slave-hunting expeditions had ravaged the Indian population.

47

Activities

Map assignment: Have students trace the routes of selected expeditions and note the various tribes encountered

Role playing: Assign roles of explorers and Indian leaders to students and act out their perception of the initial meeting between two groups: Indian and European

Instructional Aids

Filmstrip (sound): The White Man and Indians, The First Contacts (SSSS;MM)

Transparancy: Indians and Settlers (CES)

Student and Teacher Resources

See appropriate materials listed under student and teacher resources for unit six: Colonial Policies and Indian Responses

UNIT SIX
Colonial Policies and Indian Responses

Objectives

At the end of this unit, the student will be able to:

Identify:

Albany Conference	Pocahontas
Edmund Atkin	Pope's Revolt
John Eliot	Powhatan Confederacy
King Philip's War	Samoset
Lord Dunmore's War	Squanto
Massasoit	Yamasee War
Opechancanough	William Johnson
Pontiac	

Describe Puritan-Indian relations; Pilgrim-Indian relations

Distinguish between those areas and tribes most affected by early white contact with areas and tribes least or not affected

Compare and contrast the Indian policies of Spain, England, France and Netherlands

Compare and contrast the English, French, Spanish and Dutch policies toward the Indian focusing on trade relations

Describe the role of gift-giving in diplomatic relations between Indians and the French; the English

Criticize the effects of white contact on Indians

Evaluate the effects of white contact on Indian-Indian relations

Compare and contrast the response of Indians to English, French, Spanish and Dutch policies; to the colonists

Evaluate the role of the Indian in the French and Indian War in the Ohio Valley; in the Southeast

Appraise the role of William Johnson in Indian diplomacy

Describe the reaction of the Indians to the Treaty of Paris at the end of the French and Indian War; the colonists reaction to the Indians after peace

Outline

I. COLONIAL POLICIES AND ATTITUDES TOWARD THE INDIAN

    A.   Spanish
    B.   French
    C.   English
    D.   Dutch
    E.   Russia (optional)

II. INDIAN RESPONSE

    A.   Adaptation
        1.   Political Confederation
           a.   Iroquois Confederacy
           b.   Creek Confederacy
        2.   Retaliation
           a.   Pequot War
           b.   King Philip's War
           c.   Opechancanough and the Virginians
        3.   Submission
           a.   Voluntary (passive resistance)
              (1) Pueblos
           b.   Involuntary
              (1) Mission Indians

III. MISSIONARY EFFORTS

    A.   Jesuits
    B.   John Eliot

Points to Emphasize

Regional differences existed in imperial policies toward the Indian.

Differences in imperial policies toward the Indians were a reflection of differences in overall objectives of colonization.

There were various reactions and responses to the Euro-Americans by the American Indians. Many times the difference in responses can be attributed to the diverstiy of cultural backgrounds found in North American Indian tribes.

Many times colonial forces included neighboring Indian tribes thus pitting Indians against Indians. This divide-and-conquer tactic was used throughout the period of Indian-white warfare.

The concern for the "advancement" of the natives was more apparent at home than at the point of contact (Debo 1970:41).

The confusion of tongues and claims to sovereignty was compounded by the varieties of personality each (European) nation seemed to represent (Hagan 1961:2).

From King William's War in the late 17th century through the War of 1812, tribal allegiances (with European powers) were frequently dictated by the trade situation (Hagan 1961:3).

Points to Emphasize, con't.

Compared to Spanish and French, English policy was necessarily confused and contradictory, since the individual colonies contended with each other and the crown in the area of Indian affairs (Hagan 1961:9).

Each of the North American colonies in time developed its own rules and procedures for acquiring land and in other situations, often with results that endangered the colony's very existence (McNickle 1973:30).

For the Indians, both in the east and the west, there was certainly no clear indication until perhaps the late 1700's that any one of the five newcomer European nations would emerge triumphant. Until that time the view of most of the Indians seems to have been that some kind of balance of power might be struck among the warlike Europeans and themselves and that a new equilibrium of many nations would thus be established (Spicer 1969:11).

For the great majority of Indians in contact with Whites at this period (1540-1794) the major realm of adaptation was political, and the major instrument employed was the political confederation (Spicer 1969:15).

It was a period (1540-1794) of competition for trade, of forced migrations, of shifting alliances, of political instability, and of drastic cultural change (Spicer 1969:12).

Activities

Prepare a chart similar to the one on the following page and have students complete.

Divide the class into sections representing the various imperial powers in North America and present a discussion on their policy and attitudes toward the Indian. The completed chart from the above activity would prove to be a useful guide for discussion.

Discuss Debo's contention that as European territorial claims were approaching each other, Indians became "pawns in the game of imperial rivalry."

Instructional Aids

Filmstrips (silent): Chief Pontiac (EBEC)

Comparison of French, English, and Spanish Policies Toward the Indian

	French	English	Spanish
Objectives of colonial policy			
Approach to land cessions from Indians			
Intermarriage with Indians			
Missionary programs for Indians			
Trade with Indians			
Attitude toward Indian culture/ concept of the Indian			

Student and Teacher Resources

*Alden, John R.
1966   John Stuart and the Southern Colonial Frontier: A Study of Indian
        Relations, War, Trade, Land Problems in the Southern Wilderness
        (New York: Gordian Press, Inc.).

Cotterhill, Robert
1969   Southern Indians: Story of the Five Civilized Tribes Before Removal
        (Norman: University of Oklahoma Press).

Hunt, George T.
1960   Wars of the Iroquois: Study in Intertribal Trade Relations (Madison:
        University of Wisconsin Press).

Jacobs, Wilbur
1972   Dispossessing the American Indian (New York: Charles Scribner's Sons).

Jennings, Francis
1975   The Invasion of America: Indians, Colonialism and the Cant of Con-
        quest (Chapel Hill: University of North Carolina).

Johnson, F. Roy
1972   The Algonquins: History and Traditions (Murfeesboro, NC: Johnson
        Publishing Co.).

Leach, Douglas E.
1958   Flintlock and Tomahawk: New England in King Philip's War (New York:
        W.W. Norton and Co., Inc.).

McCary, Ben C.
1957   Indians in 17th Century Virginia (Charlottesville: Unversity Press
        of Virginia).

Nammack, Georgiana C.
1969   Fraud, Politics, and the Dispossession of the Indians: The Iroquois
        Land Frontier in the Colonial Period (Norman: University of Oklahoma
        Press).

Nash, Gary
1974   Red, White, and Black: The Peoples of Early America (Englewood Cliffs,
        NJ: Prentice-Hall, Inc.).

Peckham, Howard and Charles Gibson eds.
        Attitudes of the Colonial Powers Toward the American Indian
        (Salt Lake City: University of Utah Press).

Pound, Merritt
1951   Benjamin Hawkins: Indian Agent (Athens: University of Georgia Press).

Saum, Lewis O.
1966   The Fur Trader and the Indian (Seattle: University of Washington Press).

Trelease, Allen W.
1960   Indian Affairs in Colonial New York (Port Washington, New York: Kennikat
        Press, Corp.).

Student and Teacher Resources, con't.

Vaughan, Alden T.
    1965   New England Frontier: Indians and Puritans, 1620-1675 (Waltham, Mass.:
           Little, Brown and Co.).

Whipple, Chandler
    1973   The Indian and the Whiteman in Massachusetts and Rhode Island
           (Stockbridge, Mass.: Berkshire Traveller Press).

The following periodicals frequently contain articles on early Indian-White
relations and colonial policies:

    American Quarterly
    New England Quarterly
    Virginia Magazine of History
    Essex Institute Historical Collections
    William and Mary Quarterly

UNIT SEVEN

Formation of Early United States Government Indian Policy

Objectives

At the conclusion of this unit, the student will be able to:

Identify:

Alexander McGillvray   John Sullivan
Arthur St. Clair   Joseph Brant
Battle at Fallen Timbers   Lewis and Clark Expedition
Battle of Horsehoe Bend   Little Turtle
Battle of Thames   Northwest Ordinance of 1789
Benjamin Hawkins   Proclamation of 1763
Bureau of Indian Affairs   Sacajawea
Cornstalk   Tecumseh
Factory system   Treaty of Grenville
Indian Trade and Intercourse Act   William McIntosh
John Stuart   Wyoming Valley

Describe the role of the Indian in the Revolutionary War

Evaluate the effects of the Revolutionary War and the Treaty of Paris (1783) on the Indians; on the U.S. government Indian policy

Describe the role of the Indian in American diplomacy from 1783 to 1814

Describe the role of the Indian in the War of 1812

Evaluate the effects of the War of 1812 and the Treaty of Ghent (1814) on the Indians; on U.S. government Indian policy

Identify those tribes which Lewis and Clark contacted during their expedition

Analyze the Lewis and Clark expedition in terms of what it reveals about Indian-Indian relations

Describe Indian-"Mountain Men" relations

Evaluate the impact of the Louisiana Purchase on government Indian policy, in particular, on Jefferson's Indian policy

Summarize the doctrine behind Tecumseh's movement toward a Pan-Indian union

Compare and contrast the diplomatic missions of Tecumseh among the Southeastern and Northwestern tribes

Describe the federal legislative, executive and judiciary roles in the area of Indian affairs

Compare the Indian policies of Henry Knox and Thomas Jefferson

<u>Objectives</u>, con't.

Compare Jeffersonian Indian policy with that of Andrew Jackson

Evaluate Indian response to early U.S. government Indian policy

<u>Outline</u>

  I. INDIAN ROLE IN AMERICAN REVOLUTION

    A.   Attempts by tribes to remain neutral
    B.   Reasons many tribes finally sided with British
    C.   Indian response to Treaty of Paris (1783)
    D.   Effects of American Revolution on the American Indian
          1.   Case Study: The Iroquois Confederacy

 II. EARLY UNITED STATES INDIAN POLICY

    A.   Regulation of Indian Affairs: Central Government vs. the Colonies
          1.   Articles of Confederation, Article IX
    B.   Adoption of Treaty-Making Process
          1.   Delaware Treaty

III. FORMATION OF FEDERAL INDIAN POLICY

    A.   Regulation of Indian Affairs
          1.   Constitution, Article I, Section 8
          2.   Creation of Indian Department
          3.   Northwest Ordinance
                a.   Article 3
          4.   Trade and Intercourse Act
          5.   Establishment of factory system
    B.   Henry Knox and the Formation of Indian Policy under George Washington
          1.   "conquered nation" policy
                a.   reasons for its failure
          2.   Program for "civilizing" the Indian

 IV. INDIAN TREATIES AND LAND CESSIONS

    A.   Case Studies
          1.   Treaty of Holston (1791)
          2.   Treaty of Hopewell (1785)

  V. AMERICAN DIPLOMACY AND THE AMERICAN INDIAN

    A.   Jay Treaty of 1794 with Great Britain
    B.   Pinckney Treaty of 1795 with Spain

 VI. INDIAN POLICY UNDER THOMAS JEFFERSON

    A.   Expansion of Knox's policies toward "civilizing" the Indian
    B.   Effects of the Louisiana Purchase on Indian policy
          1.   Indian response to the Lewis and Clark expedition
    C.   Continued pressure for Indian lands

VII. THE AMERICAN INDIAN AND THE WAR OF 1812

    A.   Role of the Indians
          1.   Reasons many tribes again sided with Britain
    B.   Tecumseh
          1.   Plans for a Pan-Indian union
          2.   The Shawnee Prophet 56

Points to Emphasize

The role of the central government, to be played by the U.S. after the Revolution, had already assumed definite character as portrayed by the British Empire. Basically paternal in their approach to Indian problems, officials of the central government soon learned that when a conflict existed between the interests of the Indians and those of the frontiersmen, that of the Indian had to be sacrificied. (Hagan 1961:30).

After the signing of the Treaty of Ghent in 1815, the Indian had to deal solely with the American government.

Following the War of 1812, the character of Indian-American relations changed. The U.S. felt less need to conciliate the Indian nations as the threat of British intervention faded. (Hagan 1961:66).

The new phase (post-Revolutionary War) of Indian adaptation involved re-orientation, in some instances, of religious faith, in others, of political organization (Spicer 1969:47).

Activities

Handout copies of early Unites States-American Indian treaties (see Kappler, 1972). Discuss the treaty-making process, i.e., negotiations, role of government agents, interpretation of the treaties by the United States and the respective Indian tribes. How does the treaty relationship affect the legal status of Indians and Indian tribes? Compare the validity of Indian treaties to those made with foreign nations. Did the Indians fulfill their treaty obligations? Did the United States government?

Instructional Aids

Film: Andrew Jackson and the War of 1812: The Frontierman and the Indian (Learning Films, Ltd.)

Filmstrip (sound): The Role of the Indians in the American Revolution (CA)

Student and Teacher Resources

Anson, Bert
    1970   Miami Indians (Norman: University of Oklahoma Press).

Creighton, Luella B.
    1971   Tecumseh: The Story of the Shawnee Chief (New York: St. Martin's Press, Inc.).

Downes, Randolph
    1969   Council Fires on the Upper Ohio (Pittsburgh: University of Pittsburg Press).

Student and Teacher Resources, con't.

Graymont, Barbara
    1972   Iroquois in the American Revolution (New York: Syracuse University Press).

Harmon, George D.
    1941   Sixty Years of Indian Affairs, Political, Economic, and Diplomatic (Millwood, New York: Kraus Reprint Co.).

Horsman, Reginald
    1967   Expansion and American Indian Policy, 1783-1812 (Milwaukee: University of Michigan Press).

Mohr, Walter
    1933   Federal Indian Relations, 1774-1799 (St. Clair Shores, Mich.: Scholarly Press).

O'Donnell, James H.
    1973   Southern Indians in the American Revolution (Nashville: University of Tennessee Press).

Prucha, Francis P.
    1970   American Indian Policy in the Formative Years: The Indian Trade and Intercourse Acts, 1790-1834 (Lincoln: University of Nebraska Press).

Sheehan, Bernard
    1973   Seeds of Extinction: Jeffersonian Philanthropy and the American Indian (Chapel Hill: University of North Carolina Press).

Tucker, Glenn
    1973   Tecumseh: Visions of Glory (New York: Russell and Russell).

Viola, Herman T.
    1974   Thomas L. McKenney, Architect of America's Early Indian Policy, 1816-1830 (Chicago, Ill.: Swallow Press).

Weslanger, C.A.
    1972   The Delaware Indians: A History (New Brunswick, NJ: Rutgers University Press).

The following periodicals frequently contain articles on formation of early U.S. Indian policy:

    Western Pennsylvania Historical Magazine
    Wisconsin Magazine of History
    Indiana Magazine of History
    Minnesota History

In addition, see periodicals listed under student and teacher resources in unit five.

UNIT EIGHT
Revitalization Movements, East of the Mississippi

Objectives

At the conclusion of this unit, the student will be able to:

Define: revitalization movement

Identify:

    Handsome Lake
    Neolin, the Delaware Prophet
    Tenskwatawa, the Shawnee Prophet

Compare and contrast the revitalization movements of Handsome Lake, Neolin and Tenskwatawa

Outline

  I. HANDSOME LAKE

     A. Biographical sketch
     B. Foundations of his teachings
        1. Code of Handsome Lake

 II. THE ALGONAUIAN PROPHETS

     A. Neolin, the Delaware prophet
        1. Biographical sketch
        2. Foundations of his teachings
     B. The Shawnee prophet, Tenskwatawa
        1. Biographical sketch
        2. Foundations of his teachings

Points to Emphasize

Revitalization movements were just one of various Indian responses to the new conditions brought about in their contact with Whites.

The conclusions made in a comparison of revitalization movements, east of the Mississippi (see accompanying activity).

Activities

Have students complete accompanying chart comparing the three revitalization movements: Handsome Lake, the Delaware prophet, and the Shawnee prophet.

A Comparison of Revitalization Movements East of the Mississippi[1]

	HANDSOME LAKE	ALGONQUIAN PROPHETS	
		Neolin: The Delaware Prophet	Tenskawatawa: The Shawnee Prophet
General setting: background of			
Individual prophet			
Tribe (historically)			
Tribe (culturally)			
Apocalyptic Gospel			
Imminence of world destruction			
Definition of sin			
Prescription of salvation			

[1]Structured from material presented in Wallace (1972).

	HANDSOME LAKE	ALGONQUIAN PROPHETS	
		Neolin: The Delaware Prophet	Tenskawatawa: The Shawnee Prophet
Social Gospel			
Moral regeneration			
Land retention			
Domestic morality			
Peace and social unity			
Acculturation			
Attitudes toward whites, in gen'l.			
Attitudes toward white culture			

	HANDSOME LAKE	ALGONQUIAN PROPHETS	
		Neolin: The Delaware Prophet	Tenskawatawa: The Shawnee Prophet
Attitudes toward missionaries			
Outcome of movement			
Summary			

Conclusions:

Optional categories:

Instructional Aids

Student and Teacher Resources

*Mooney, James
    1912   "Prophets" (in <u>Handbook of American Indians, North of Mexico</u>, Frederick W. Hodge, ed., Westport, Conn.: Greenwood Press, Inc.).

*Parker, Anthony C.
    1968   <u>Parker on the Iroquois</u> (includes Code of Handsome Lake, the Seneca Prophet) (New York: Syracuse University Press).

Wallace, Anthony F.C.
    1972   <u>The Death and Rebirth of the Seneca</u> (Westminster, Md.: Random House, Inc.).

*   1956   <u>Revitalization Movements</u> (American Anthropologist, col. 58, pp. 264-281).

UNIT NINE
Indian Removal

Objectives

At the conclusion of this unit, students will be able to:

Identify:

Andrew Jackson	Major Ridge
Black Hawk	Osceola
Cherokee Nation vs. Georgia	Samuel Worcester
Cherokee Pheonix	Sequoyah
Elias Boudinot	Tsali
Governor Gilmer	"Trail of Tears"
Indian Codes	Treaty of Echota
Indian Removal Act	Treaty Party
John Marshall	Wilson Lumpkin
John Ridge	Worcester vs. State of Georgia
John Ross	1802 Compact

Compare and contrast, in depth, the removals of the Creek, Cherokee, Chickasaw, Choctaw, and Seminole

Appraise the effects of Cherokee Nation and Worcester on the legal status of Indian tribes

Judge Jandrew Jackson's reaction to the Supreme Court's decision on Worcester vs. State of Georgia

Explain the intratribal rift between the "Treaty Party" and those opposed to removal

Propose alternatives to Indian removal

Compare and contrast the displacement of the Northwestern tribes to the removal of the "Five Civilized Tribes"

Describe the relations between the "removed" Indian population in Indian territory with neighboring tribes

Describe the adjustments the tribes had to make to their new home

Judge whether Indian removal was part of "Manifest Destiny" or "National Dishonor"

Describe what Edward Spicer called the "Cherokee Renaissance"

<u>Outline</u>

I. ORIGINS OF INDIAN REMOVAL

II. INDIAN REMOVAL POLICY UNDER ANDREW JACKSON
    A. Attitudes of Jackson toward the American Indian
       1. Experiences in "Red Stick" (Creek) was
       2. Philosophy toward aboriginal Indian land title
    B. Indian Removal Act on May 28, 1830
    C. Removal of the "Five Civilized Tribes"
       1. Choctaws, 1830-1831
       2. Creeks, 1831
       3. Cherokees, Summer 1838
       4. Chickasaws, Winter 1837-1838
       5. Seminoles, 1846
         a. Seminole wars
    D. The Northern Tribes and Indian Removal
       1. Osage removed to Kansas, 1831
       2. Indians removed from new states of Missouri, Arkansas and Iowa
       3. Black Hawk War, 1831-1832
         a. Sauk and Fox tribes resisted removal under the leadership of
           Black Hawk

III. CASE STUDY: THE REMOVAL OF THE CHEROKEE NATION
    A. The Cherokee's cultural "renaissance"
    B. Increased pressure from Georgia for Cherokee lands
       1. 1802 compact with Federal government
       2. Discovery of gold on Cherokee lands
       3. Continual encroachment by white settlers
    C. Cherokees Take Their Case to Court
       1. Gerogia extends state jurisdiction over Cherokee lands
         a. Denies civil rights to Cherokees
         b. Voids all Cherokee laws
       2. Cherokee Nation brings suit against state of Georgia in the Supreme Court
         a. Cherokee Nation vs. Georgia
           (1) Reason case rejected by Marshall
       3. Worcester vs. State of Georgia
         a. Court declares extension of Georgia laws over Cherokees unconsti-
           tutional
         b. Indian tribes are "dependent domestic nations"
         c. Jackson's reply to Marchalls' decision
    D. Intratribal Split over Issue of Removal
    E. The "Trail of Tears"

<u>Points to Emphasize</u>

The notion that northern tribes, as well as the "Five Civilized" tribes were victims
of removal

The justification used for removing the other tribes in the Southeast could not
be used in attempting to rationalize the removal of the Cherokee

Points to Emphasize, con't.

The ramifications of Indian removal on intratribal and intertribal relations

While agreement to removal supposedly was voluntary, pressure was applied by the federal and state governments. The encroachment of Indian lands was encouraged. In this type of atmosphere, the Indians were forced into signing removal treaties.

The Indians, in many instances, had the option of remaining and accepting individual plots of land. However, through fradulent practices, they lost their tracts of land and followed their displaced kinsmen.

Proponents of removal were numerous and vocal. It was apparent that contact with the average frontiersman was not an elevating experience for the Indian. Thus, it could be argued that removal would make possible quarantining the Indian until he could assimilate enough civilization to take his place in white society. (Hagan 1961:68).

Sectionalism entered the debate over Indian removal policy.

Activities

Have students assume roles of the leading figures, Indian and white, in the dispute over Indian removal. Divide into two groups-those supporting removal and those opposed to it.

As an alternative to the above activity, simply have class present a panel discussion on the pros and cons of Indian removal.

Panel discussion on the role of Andrew Jackson and Indian policy.

Have students present oral or written reports on leading Indian figures during this period.

Have students write a newspaper account of the "Trail of Tears."

Instructional Aids

Film: Sequoyah (Disney)

Cassette: Florida and the Seminoles (EDC)
             The Trail of Tears (EDC)

Transparency: Trail of Tears (CES)

Student and Teacher Resources

*Abel, Annie H.
    1908   History of Events Resulting in Indian Consolidation West of the
            Mississippi (New York: AMS Press, Inc.).

Student and Teacher Resources, con't.

Bass, Althea
    1968   Cherokee Messenger: The Life of Samuel Arthur Worcester (Norman:
            University of Oklahoma Press).

Collier, Peter
    1973   When Shall They Rest? The Cherokees' Long Struggle with America
            (New York: Dell Publishing Co., Inc.).

Debo, Angie
    1961   Road to Disappearance: A History of the Creek Indians (Norman:
            University of Oklahoma Press).

    1966   And Still Waters Run: The Betrayal of the Five Civilized Tribes (New
            Jersey: Princeton University Press).

    1972   Rise and Fall of the Choctaw Nation (Norman: University of Oklahoma
            Press).

DeRosier, Arthur
    1970   Removal of the Choctaw Indians (Nashville: University of Tennessee Press).

Filler, Louis and Allen Guttmann eds.
    1962   Removal of the Cherokee Nation: Manifest Destiny or National Dishonor
            (Lexington, Mass.: D.C. Heath and Co.).

Foreman, Grant
    1946   Last Trek of the Indians (New York: Russell and Russell).

    1968   Advancing the Frontier, 1830-1860 (Norman: University of Oklahoma Press).

    1971   Five Civilized Tribes (Norman: University of Oklahoma Press).

    1972   Indian Removal: The Emigration of the Five Civilized Tribes of
            Indians (Norman: University of Oklahoma Press).

Holland, James W.
    1969   Andrew Jackson and the Creek War: Victory at Horseshoe (University:
            University of Alabama Press).

Jackson, Donald ed.
    1964   Black Hawk: An Autobiography (Urbana: University of Illinois Press).

Jahoda, Gloria
    1975   The Trail of Tears: The Story of the American Indian Removals, 1813-
            1855 (New York: Holt, Rinehart, and Winston).

Jordon, Jan
    1973   Give Me the Wind: A Biographical Novel of John Ross, Chief of the
            Cherokee (Englewood Cliffs, NJ: Prentice-Hall, Inc.).

Malone, Henry
    1956   Cherokees of the Old South: A People in Transition (Athens: University
            of Georgia Press).

Student and Teacher Resources, con't.

McReynolds, Edwin C.
     1972   The Seminoles (Norman: University of Oklahoma Press).

*Rogin, Michael Paul
     1975   Father and Children: Andrew Jackson and the Subjugation of the
             American Indian (Westminster, Md.: Alfred A. Knopf, Inc.).

Royce, Charles C.
     1975   The Cherokee Nation of Indians (Chicago: Aldine Publishing Co.).

Satz, Ronald N.
     1974   American Indian Policy in the Jacksonian Era (Lincoln: University of
             Nebraska Press).

Starkey, Marion L.
     1946   Cherokee Nation (New York: Russell and Russell).

Van Every, Dale
     1967   Disinherited (New York: Avon Books).

Wilkins, Thurman
     1970   Cherokee Tragedy (New York: Macmillan Publishing Co.).

Williams, Jeanne
     1972   Trail of Tears: American Indians Driven From Their Lands (New York:
             G.P. Putnam's Sons).

Woodward, Grace
     1964   Cherokees (Norman: University of Oklahoma Press).

Young, Mary
     1961   Redskins, Riffleshirts, and Rednecks: Indian Allotments in Georgia
             and Mississippi, 1830-1860 (Norman: University of Oklahoma Press).

The following periodicals frequently contain articles on Indian removal and
Southern Indian relations:

     Georgia Historical Quarterly
     Florida Historical Quarterly
     Journal of Southern History
     Tennessee Historical Quarterly
     Chronicles of Oklahoma

UNIT TEN
Intertribal Relations on the Plains

Objectives
=========

At the conclusion of this unit, the student will be able to:

Compare trade goods in various stages of Plains trade

Appraise the effects of the horse on patterns of trade on the Plains

Summarize relationships established among Plains tribes through trade

Construct a map showing intertribal trade on the Upper Missouri before Lewis and Clark

Describe Plains Indian relations with removed and dispossessed tribes

Outline
=======

I.   BUILDING A NEW HOME: "DISPOSSESSED" AND "REMOVED" TRIBES ON THE PLAINS

    A. The Five Civilized Tribes
       1. Efforts to reestablish pre-removal developments
       2. Relations with Plains tribes
    B. "Displaced" Algonquian tribes on the Plains
       1. Case Studies: Delaware, Kickapoos, and the Fox[1]
       2. Relations with surrounding tribes

II. INTERTRIBAL TRADE ON THE UPPER MISSOURI[2]

    A. Aboriginal Intertribal Trade Patterns
       1. Trading centers
       2. Flow of goods
       3. Types of goods exchanged
    B. Protohistoric (or Transitional) Trade Pattern
       1. Introduction of articles of European origin
          a. Effects on aboriginal trade pattern
    C. Direct Historic Trade Between Indians and Whites
       1. Fur trade
       2. Effects of Lewis and Clark expedition on aboriginal trade pattern
    D. Case Study: The Cheyenne in Plains Indian trade[3]

Points to Emphasize
===================

"Dispossessed" and "removed" tribes did not move into a vacuum on the Plains

The study of trade relations, between Indian-Indian and Indian-White, offers an alternative view of Plains history other than its more militant aspects

Points to Emphasize, con't.

Through the medium of trade relationships, Plains tribes established peace among themselves to present a more unified front to the onslaught of settlers, Indian and white

As early as 1816 clashes were occurring between the Western tribes and the migrating Indians...Much of the fighting that went on does not substantiate the reputation of the plains tribesmen as the fiercest warriors on the continent. Better armed, the eastern Indians more than held their own. (Hagan 1961:86)

Activities

Using Ewer's article, "The Indian Trade of the Upper Missouri before Lewis and Clark: An Interpretation", as guide, have students complete chart on page 72.

Role-playing: Have students act out an initial meeting between leaders of a Plains tribe and members of a removed tribe.

Instructional Aids

Maps: (1) Intertribal trade on the Upper Missouri before Lewis and Clark (Ewers 1954:441)
(2) Influx of the horse on the Plains

Film: Catlin and the Indians (McGraw-Hill)

Student and Teacher Resources

Boller, Henry
      1972   Among the Indians: Four Years on the Upper Missouri, 1858-1862 (Lincoln: University of Nebraska Press).

Denig, Edwin T.
      1961   Five Indian Tribes of the Upper Missouri: Sioux, Arickaras, Assiniboines, Crees and Crows (Norman: University of Oklahoma Press).

Ewers, John
      1955   Blackfeet: Raiders on the Northwestern Plains(Norman: University of Oklahoma Press).

      1968   Indian Life on the Upper Missouri (Norman: University of Oklahoma Press).

      1954   The Indian Trade of the Upper Missouri before Lewis and Clark (Missouri Historical Society Bulletin, vol. 10, pp.429-446).

Fahey, John
      1974   The Flathead Indians (Norman: University of Oklahoma Press).

Student and Teacher Resources, con't.

Gregg, Josiah
    1958   Commerce of the Prairies (Norman: University of Oklahoma Press).

Hyde, George
    1959   Indians of the High Plains: From the Prehistoric Period to the
            Coming of the Europeans (Norman: University of Oklahoma Press).

*Jablow, Joseph
    1951   Cheyenne in Plains Indian Trade Relations, 1795-1840 (Seattle:
            University of Washington Press).

McNitt, Frank
    1972   The Indian Traders (Norman: University of Oklahoma Press).

Mayhall, Mildred
    1972   Kiowas (Norman: University of Oklahoma Press).

See periodicals listed under student and teacher resources for units eleven and
twelve.

A Comparison of Goods in Various Stages of Plains Trade

	Agricultural Tribes	Nomadic Plains Tribes	Whites
Aboriginal Intertribal Trade Pattern			XXXXXXXXX
Protohistoric (or Transitional) Trade			
Direct Historic Trade			

For each pattern, draw arrows showing the flow of trade goods between categories.

FOOTNOTES

[1] See Spicer (1969), pages 77-82.

[2] Based upon Ewers (1954).

[3] See Jablow (1950).

UNIT ELEVEN
Conquest and Confinement: The Plains

Objectives

At the conclusion of this unit, the student will be able to:

Identify:

Black Kettle	Kicking Bird
Colonel John Chivington	Little Crow
Crazy Horse	Medicine Lodge Treaty of 1867
Dull Knife	Quanah Parker
Gall	Red Cloud
George Bent	Roman Nose
George Custer	Santanta
General Wm. T. Sherman	Spotted Tail
General Hancock	Ft. Laramie Treaty of 1866

Summarize major Indian battles on the Plains

Synthesize and analyze major confrontations on the Plains in selected areas

Describe conditions found on early reservations and Indian responses to those conditions

Outline

I. MAJOR CONFRONTATIONS ON THE PLAINS[1]

    A. Northern Plains
        1. Sioux "Uprising" of 1862
        2. Red Cloud and the Bozeman Trail
           a. Fetterman Massacre
        3. Battle of Little Big Horn
        4. The Ghost Dance and the Wounded Knee Massacre
    B. Central Plains
        1. Cheyenne-Arapaho war, 1864-1865
        2. Flight of the Cheyenne, 1879
        3. Sand Creek Massacre
    C. Southern Plains
        1. Battle of Beecher Island
        2. Attack on the Washita: another Sand Creek
        3. Red River War
    D. Break in the action, 1861-1865: The Indian role in the Civil War
        1. The Five Civilized Tribes and the Confederacy

II. CONFINEMENT: LIFE ON A RESERVATION

    A. Arguments for and against the establishment of reservations
    B. Survey of Indian reservations established
    C. Effects of Reservation Life on the Indian

    1. Changes (if any) in social organization, political organization,
        subsistence patterns, religion, and personality
D. Indian response to reservation life
    1. Passive
    2. Active
E. Case study
F. Establishment of Boarding Schools
    1. Carlisle

Points to Emphasize

In many instances, "massacres" of whites by the Indians were simply a case of the
military being outwitted and hopelessly outnumbered (Andrist 1969:122).

Effects of the depletion of the buffalo herds on the Plains Indians.

The reservation system under which Indians continued to live influenced profoundly
all aspects of Indian life, especially their social and political organization.
The changes did not come about in precisely the same way on all reservations. Differences in administrative technique and differences in the nature of the varied
Indian societies resulted in a remarkable variety of results. (Spicer 1969:100)

This theater of war (referring to the Plains) was very different from those which
had developed east of the Mississippi. Not only was there no complicating multi-
plicity of European nations, but also the Sioux Council Fires were much less
centralized than even the Creek Confederacy or the League of the Iroquois. (Spicer
1969:85)

The reservation system of administrative control stimulated the growth of political
issues, but suppressed the means for settling them. Political power for decision-
making remained in the hands of the superintendent. Lacking mechanisms for re-
solving differences, the Indian communities became pervaded with factional strife
under the surface of imposed order. (Spicer 1969:111)

Activities

Written report: Biography of an Indian leader

Have students write a paper on the following topics: (1) Diary entry of an American
soldier on the frontier participating in the wars with the Indins; (2) An Indian
warrior recounting his war exploits to his friends; (3) Journalist describing an
Indian battle.

Compare and contrast an Indian version of a famous battle with a version from a
newspaper or military report at that time.

Have students complete a synthesis of selected battles. See accompanying guide on
page 74.

Map Assignment: (1) Locate major battle sites, noting tribes involved and year; (2)
Compare the above completed assignment with a map showing expansion of the frontier.
What conclusions can be drawn?

Instructional Aids

Films: Now That the Buffalo's Gone (Pyramid)
                    Red Sunday (Little Big Horn) (Pyramid)
                    Glory Trail: The Mighty Warrior(Illinois)
                    Report from Wounded Knee (Oregon; Illinois)
                    Gone West (Time-Life)
                    End of the Trail, parts one and two (Minnesota)
                    Age of the Buffalo (Minnesota)
                    How the West Was Won...and Honor Lost (Berkeley, Minnesota, Illinois,
                        Indiana, Oregon, McGraw-Hill)

Photo Aids: The Indians of the Plains-Strangers in Their Own Land (SSSS)

Record: Red Hawk's Account of Custer's Last Battle (SSSS)

Filmstrips: Sitting Bull: Tatankaiyotake (SSSS)
(sound)   Indian Viewpoint series (SSSS)
                    Indian Words From the End of the Trail (SSSS; MM)
                    The Sioux: As Long As the Grass Grows and the Water Flows (PF)
                    Sitting Bull and Chief Joseph (SW Film Center)
                    Plenty Coups and Pretty Shield (SW Film Center)

Cassette: Bury My Heart at Wounded Knee (A_T)
                    The Sioux Indians and Custer (EDC)

Transparency: Custer's Last Stand (CES)

Discussion questions for Chapters 10, 12 and 13

The central focus of these chapters is the conflict between Indians and whites
on the frontier. While the majority of these engagements were on the Northern and
Southern Plains, California and the Northwest were also subject to similar pres-
sures and strife.

For a better perspective in analyzing these confrontations, summarize the major
battles using these categories: Date(s); leading Indian tribe(s) and leaders;
American participants, both military and non-military; reasons which precipitated
the outbreak; Indian's reaction; white's reaction; and eventual outcome. Example:

SIOUX "UPRISING" IN MINNESOTA, 1862

LEADING TRIBE(S): Santee Sioux

LEADERS: Little Crow (Indian); Henry Sibley (Major American Figure)

REASONS: Grievances by Indians over frontier encroachment and rigged treaties. In
         addition, trader's debts were inflated and annuity money was deflated.
         Whites angered by the killing of a few residents by a few irresponsible
         young Indians.

INDIAN REACTION: Fearing reprisal, struck out at nearby settlements

WHITE REACTION: Organization of a military unit to protect and defend white
         residents of state.

EVENTUAL OUTCOME: Indians beaten; 38 Siuox hanged; others placed on a reservation

Discussion questions, con't.

       in Nebraska; ex-reservation in Minnesota "wiped off map."

Once you have completed this synthesis, analyze your findings and construct a distinct pattern these wars seemed to imitate.

Student and Teacher Resources

*Abel, Annie H.
    1919   American Indian as Participant in The Civil War (New York: Johnson Reprint Corp.).

Adams, Alexander
    1973   Sitting Bull: A Biography (New York: B.P. Putnam's Sons).

Ambrose, Stephen E.
    1975   Crazy Horse and Custer (New York: Doubleday and Company, Inc.).

*Bailey, Thomas M.
    1972   Reconstruction in Indian Territory (Port Washington, New York: Kennikat Press, Corp.).

Brady, Cyrus, T.
    1971   Indian Fights and Fighters (Lincoln: University of Nebraska Press).

Brown, Dee
    1972   Bury My Heart at Wounded Knee: An Indian History of the American West (New York: Bantam Books, Inc.).

    1972   The Fetterman Massacre (London: Barrie and Jenkins, Ltd.).

    1974   Fighting Indians of the West (Westminster, MD.: Ballantine Books, Inc.).

Danziger, Edmund J., Jr.
    1974   Indians and Bureaucrats: Administering the Reservation Policy During the Civil War (Urbana: University of Illinois Press).

Dixon, Joseph
    1972   The Vanishing Race (New York: Popular Library, Inc.).

Ellis, Richard N.
    1970   General Pope and United States Indian Policy (Albuquerque: University of New Mexico Press).

Fischer, LeRoy H. ed.
    1974   The Civil War Era in Indian Territory (Los Angeles, CA: Lorren L. Morrison, Publisher).

Grinnell, George
    1956   Fighting Cheyennes (Norman: University of Oklahoma Press).

Hagan, William
    1966   Indian Police and Judges: Experiments in Acculturation and Control

Student and Teacher Resources, con't.

>(New Haven, Conn.: Yale University Press).

Haines, Francis
>1970   Buffalo (New York: Thomas Y. Crowell Co.).

Hoig, Stan
>1961   Sand Creek Massacre (Norman: University of Oklahoma Press).

Jones, Douglas C.
>1974   Treaty of Medicine Lodge (Norman: University of Oklahoma Press).

Knight, Oliver
>1960   Following the Indian Wars: The Story of Newspaper Correspondents Among
>the Indian Campaigners (Norman: University of Oklahoma Press).

Lame Deer and Richard Erodos
>1972   Lame Deer: Seeker of Visions (New York: Simon and Schuster, Inc.).

Linderman, Frank B.
>1972   Plenty-Coups, Chief of the Crows (New York: John Day Co., Inc.).

Marshall, S.L.A.
>1972   Crimsoned Prarie (New York: Charles Scribner's Sons).

Meyer, Roy
>1967   History of the Santee Sioux: United States Indian Policy on Trial
>(Lincoln: University of Nebraska Press).

Neihardt, John
>1972   Black Elk Speaks (New York: Pocket Books, Inc.).

Nye, William S.
>1968   Plains Indian Raiders: The Final Phase of Warfare from the Arkansas
>to the Red River (Norman: University of Oklahoma Press).

Olson, James
>1965   Red Cloud and the Sioux Problem (Lincoln: University of Nebraska Press).

Sandoz, Mari
>1961   Crazy Horse: The Strange Man of the Oglalas; a Biography (Lincoln:
>University of Nebraska Press).

Smith, Rex Alan
>1975   Moon of Popping Trees (New York: Reader's Digest Press).

Standing Bear, Luther
>1975   My People the Sioux (Lincoln: University of Nebraska Press).

Terrell, John Upton
>1972   Land Grab: The Truth About the Winning of the West (New York: Dial Press).

Trennert, Robert A., Jr.
>1975   Alternatives to Extinction: Federal Indian Policy and the Beginnings

Student and Teacher Resources, con't.

of the Reservation System, 1846-1851 (Philadelphia: Temple University Press).

Utley, Robert
1963   Last Days of the Sioux Nation (New Haven, Conn.: Yale University Press).

1974   Frontier Regulars: The United States Army and the Indian, 1866 to 1890 (New York: Macmillan Publishing Co., Inc.).

Webb, Walter Prescott
1931   The Great Plains (New York: Grossett and Dunlap, Inc.).

Wellman, Paul
1954   The Indian Wars of the West (Garden City, New York: Doubleday and Company, Inc.).

White, Lonnie ed.
1972   Hostiles and Horse Soldiers (Boulder, Colo: Pruett Publishing Co.).

Wissler, Clark
1971   Red Man Reservations (New York: Macmillan Publishing Co., Inc.).

The following periodicals frequently contain articles on Plains Indians relations and reservation life:

American West
Annals of Wyoming
Colorado Magazine
Great Plains Journal
Journal of the West
Montana
Nebraska History
North Dakota History
South Dakota History
Southwestern Historical Quarterly
Western Historical Quarterly
Chronicles of Oklahoma

FOOTNOTES

[1]Compiled from Andrist, 1969 and Brown, 1972.

UNIT TWELVE
Conquest and Confinement-The Far West

Objectives

At the conclusion of this unit, the student will be able to:

Identify:

Captain Jack   Henry Spaulding
Cheif Joseph   Issac Stevens
Chief Washaskie   John Clum
Council of Walla Walla   Manuelito
General Crook   Marcus Whitman
General Howard   Tom Jeffords
Geronimo   Victorio

Outline

I. CONQUEST: THE FAR WEST

    A. Northwest
        1. Retreat of Chief Joseph
        2. Bannock War
    B. California
        1. Mission system, effects of
        2. Indian response to Spanish and Mexican policies
        3. Captain Jack and the Modoc War
    C. Southwest
        1. Treaty of Guadalupe-Hidalgo
        2. The Long Walk of the Navajos
        3. Campaigns against the Apache

II. RESERVATION LIFE

    A. Northwest
        1. Establishment of Missions
        2. Case study
    B. California
        1. Unratified Treaties
        2. Case study
    C. The Southwest
        1. Case study

Points to Emphasize

Activities

Have students complete a synthesis of selected battles. See accompanying guide on page 76 . Substitute a far western battle for your example.

Instructional Aids

Films: Long Walk (Berkeley)
           Ishi (Berkeley)

Cassette: Ishi In Two Worlds, part one and part two (A-T)

Student and Teacher Resources

Barrett, S.M. ed.
     1970   Geronimo: His Own Story (New York: E.P. Dutton and Co., Inc.).

Beals, Merrill D.
     1969   I Will Fight No More Forever: Chief Joseph and the Nez Perce War
            (Seattle: University of Washington Press).

Brown, Mark
     1972   The Flight of the Nez Perce (New York: G.P. Putnam's Sons).

Dillon, Richard H.
     1973   Burnt-Out Fires: California's Modoc Indian War (Englewood Cliffs, NJ:
            Prentice-Hall, Inc.).

Dunn, J.P.
     1969   Massacres of the Mountains: A History of Indian Wars of the Far West,
            1815-1875 (New York: G.P. Putnam's Sons).

Faulk, Odie B.
     1969   The Geronimo Campaign (New York: Oxford University Press).

     1974   Crimson Desert: Indian Wars of the American Southwest (New York:
            Oxford University Press).

Foreman, Grant
     1936   Indians and Pioneers: The Story of the American Southwest before 1830
            (Norman: University of Oklahoma Press).

Heizer, Robert
     1972   They Were Only Diggers (Ramona, CA: Ballena Press).

Heizer, Robert F. ed.
     1974   The Destruction of the California Indians (Salt Lake City, Utah:
            Peregrine Smith, Inc.).

*Hoopes, A.W.
     1932   Indian Affairs and Their Administration, with Special Reference to the
            Far West (Millwood, New York: Kraus Reprint Co.).

Howard, Helen and Dan L. McGrath
     1964   War Chief Joseph (Lincoln: University of Nebraska Press).

Josephy, Alvin M., Jr.
     1971   Nez Perce and the Opening of the Northwest (New Haven, Conn.: Yale
            University Press).

Student and Teacher Resources, con't.

Kroeber, Theodora
    1961   Ishi in Two Worlds: A Biographer of the Last Wild Indian in North
            America (Berkeley: University of California Press).

Mails, Thomas
    1974   The People Called Apache (Englewood Cliffs, NJ: Prentice-Hall, Inc.).

Phillips, George
    1975   Chiefs and Challengers: Indian Resistance and Cooperation in Southern
            California (Berkeley: University of California Press).

Schellie, Don
    1971   Vast Domain of Blood (New York: Tower Publications, Inc.).

Spicer, Edward H.
    1962   Cycles of Conquest: The Impact of Spain, Mexico, and the United
            States on Indians of the Southwest, 1533-1960 (Tucson: University of
            Arizona Press).

Terrell, John Upton
    1974   Apache Chronicle (New York: Apollo Editions).

Weems, John Edward
    1976   Death Song: The Last of the Indian Wars (New York: Doubleday and
            Company, Inc.).

The following periodicals frequently contain articles on Indian affairs in the
Far West:
    Californai Historical Quarterly
    Journal of Arizona History
    Nevada Historical Society Quarterly
    New Mexico Historical Review
    Oregon Historical Quarterly
    Pacific Northwest Quarterly

UNIT THIRTEEN

Revitalization Movements, West of the Mississippi and the Peyote Religion

Objectives

At the conclusion of this unit, the student will be able to:

Identify:

> Ghost Dance
> Ghost Dance shirts
> The Native American Church
> Prophet Dance
> Smohalla
> Wovoka

Compare and contrast the revitalization movements of Smohalla and Wovoka

Compare and contrast revitalization movements, east of the Mississippi, to those which rose in the West

Outline

> I. SMOHALLA AND THE PROPHET DANCE
>
>> A. Biographical sketch
>> B. Foundations of his teachings
>
> II. WOVOKA AND THE GHOST DANCE
>
>> A. Biographical sketch
>> B. Foundations of his teachings
>> C. Adoption or rejection by various tribes
>>> 1. Case study: The Sioux
>
> III. THE PEYOTE RELIGION
>
>> A. Origins of the Peyote religion
>> B. The Peyote rite
>> C. The Native American Church

Points to Emphasize

Many tribes rejected the "message" of Wovoka while others either adopted it wholly or adapted his teachings to their physical and cultural needs.

The kind of religious revelation which moved the Algonquians and gave a powerful ideology to Tecumseh's resistance in the early nineteenth century appeared again in the late 1800's among the plains and the mountain people of the west. It arose under similar circumstances (my underlines). (Spicer 1969:88)

<u>Points to Emphasize</u>, con't.

The Peyote religion is a syncretism of traditional Indian religion and Christianity.

<u>Activities</u>

Have students complete the chart on "A Comparative Analysis of Revitalization Movements, West of the Mississippi" on the following pages.

<u>Instructional Aids</u>

Records: <u>Washo-Peyote Songs</u> (Folkways Records)
             "Peyote Cult Dance" on <u>Music of the Sioux and Navajo</u> (Folkways Records)

<u>Student and Teacher Resources</u>

Barnett, Homer
    1957   <u>Messianic Cult Indian Shakers: of the Pacific Northwest</u> (Carbondale: Southern Illinois University Press).

LaBarre, Weston
    1970   <u>The Ghost Dance</u> (New York: Dell Publishing Company, Inc.).

    1972   <u>The Peyote Cult</u> (New York: Schoken Books).

Marriott, Alice and Carol K. Rachlin
    1972   <u>Peyote</u> (New York: New American Library, Inc.).

*Mooney, James
    1912   "Prophets" and "Smohalla" (in <u>Handbook of American Indians, North of Mexico</u>, Frederick W. Hodge, ed., Westport, Conn.: Greenwood Press, Inc.).

    1965   <u>Ghost Dance Religion and the Sioux Outbreak of 1890</u> (Chicago: University of Chicago Press).

Slotkin, James
    1956   <u>The Peyote Religion: A Study in Indian-White Relations</u> (Glencoe, Ill.: The Free Press).

A Comparative Analysis of Revitalization Movements,
West of the Mississippi[1]

	Smohalla and the Prophet Dance	Wovoka and the Ghost Dance	
General setting: background of			
Individual prophet			
Tribe (historically)			
Tribe (culturally)			
Apocalyptic Gospel			
Imminence of world destruction			
Definition of sin			
Presciption of salvation			

[1]Structured from material presented in Wallace (1972).

	Smohalla and the Prophet Dance	Wovoka and the Ghost Dance	
Social Gospel:			
Moral regeneration			
Land retention			
Domestic morality			
Peace and social unity			
Acculturation:			
Attitudes toward whites, in gen'l.			
Attitudes toward white culture			

	Smohalla and the Prophet Dance	Wovoka and the Ghost Dance	
attitudes toward missionaries			
Outcome of movement			
Summary			

Conclusions:

Optional categories:

UNIT FOURTEEN
Breaking up the Reservation-The Dawes Act

Objectives

At the conclusion of this unit, the student will be able to:

Identify:

Appropriation Act of 1871   Burke Act
Curtis Act   Dawes Commission
Dawes Act (General Allotment Act)
"restricted Indian"
Richard Pratt
Jerome Commission
Henry Dawes

Describe the methods used in breaking down traditional communal ownership of the Indian lands

Compare and contrast the arguments for breaking up the reservations

Summarize the major features of the Dawes Act

Evaluate the Indian's reaction to the Dawes Act

Describe the complicated process of removing intruders from Indian lands

Describe the methods used by grafters, government officials, and guardians to liquidate the land holdings of the Indians

Evaluate attempts by Congress to compensate the Indians for their losses

Appriase the effects of the Dawes Act

Judge whether it was a success or failure

Outline

I.   RESERVATION LIFE

    A.   Reaction to Reservation Life by Indians
    B.   Effects of reservation life on Indian culture
       1.   Erosion of political rights
       2.   Loss of self-determination
    C.   Role of boarding schools

II. BREAKING UP THE RESERVATIONS-THE GENERAL ALLOTMENT ACT

    A.   Debate over bill
    B.   Provisions of the Dawes Act
    C.   Case Studies
    D.   Failure of the Dawes Act

Points to Emphasize

Boarding schools were conceived in terms of driving a wedge between children and parents thus hastening the process of cultural assimilation. (Spicer 1969:116)

So long as the Indian tribes could hold the policy-makers at arm's length, as they managed to do through the treaty process, they could determine for themselves what internal controls they chose to exercise over land or other community interests. With that barrier breached in 1871, only the judicial process remained as a defense against encroachment. (McNickle 1973:79)

...since 1871 it has been United States policy to legislate in Indian matters, not to negotiate, often not even to consult, no matter what effect the legislation might have on the civil and property rights of the Indians. The policy (Appropriation Act for 1871) enactment was the recognition of a reality-that Indian friendship and support were no longer needed by the nation come to power. (McNickle 1973:77)

It was not the gold miners or the railway promoters who appeared in the halls of Congress or wrote articles for the press in support of the measure (General Allotment Act). The advocacy, often emotionally charged, came from responsible public officials, from civic and religious bodies, and from organizations chartered to promote and protect Indian interests. (McNickle 1973:80-81)

By 1887 all the Indians west of the Mississippi had been, with the exception of most of the Papagos of southern Arizona, brought under the reservation system of control. The objective of the new policy as exemplified in the General Allotment Act was ultimately to eliminate reservations and merge Indians in the general population. (Spicer 1969:100)

The allotment program...had turned out to have reverse effects from those desired, namely, the creation of many new trust responsibilities which the federal government felt it necessary to assume in order to prevent complete disaster for Indians. It was complex, requiring additional new staff for the Bureau of Indian Affairs as it went into the business of trust management of individual property. (Spicer 1969: 113)

Between 1887 and 1934 the Indians were separated from an estimated 86,000,000 of a total of 138,000,000 acres. Most of that remaining was desert or semidesert: worthless to the white population. (Hagan 1961:147)

Activities

Panel discussion on the pros and cons of the Dawes Act

Instructional Aids

Student and Teacher Resources

Mardock, Robert W.
   1971   Reformers and the American Indian (Columbia, MO.: University of Missouri Press).

Otis, Delos S.
   1973   The Dawes Act and the Allotment of Indian Lands (Norman: University of Oklahoma Press).

Priest, Loring B.
   1969   Uncle Sam's Stepchildren: The Reformation of United States Indian Policy, 1865-1887 (New York: Octagon Books).

Prucha, Francis D.
   1973   Americanizing the American Indians: Writings by the Friends of the Indian, 1880-1900 (Cambridge, Mass.: Harvard University Press).

Washburn, Wilson E. ed.
   1975   The Assault on Indian Tribalism: The General Allotment Law (Dawes Act) (Philadelphia, Penn.: J.P. Lippincott Co.).

UNIT FIFTEEN
Indian Reform and the Indian Reorganization Act

Objectives

At the conclusion of this unit, the student will be able to:

Identify:

Charles Eastman	Johnson-O'Malley Act
Charles Rhoads	Josehp Scattergood
Dr. W. Carson Ryan	John Collier
Felix Cohen	Meriam Report
Helen Hunt Jackson	National Congress of American Indians
Indian Citizenship Act	Pueblo Land Bill/Bursum Bill
Indian Health Service	Lake Mohonk Conferences
Ira Hayes	
Indian Reorganization Act	

Summarize the reforms implemented by the Rhoads-Scattergood-Ryan tripartite during the Hoover administration

Describe the major provisions of the Indian Reorganization Act

Compare and contrast the philosophy of John Collier to that of the supporters of the Dawes Act

Evaluate the criticisms leveled against the reform policies of Collier

Summarize the educational, economic, and administrative reforms during Collier's term as Indian Commissioner

Describe the efforts undertaken to consolidate Indian land holdings

Evaluate the success of the Indian Reorganization Act

Evaluate the effects of off-reservation work during World War II

Outline

I.   INDIAN REFORM MOVEMENTS: POST ALLOTMENT
    A.   Formation of philanthropic groups interested in the welfare of the Indians
       1.   Mohonk Conferences
       2.   Association of American Indian Affairs
       3.   Indian Rights Association

II. PRE-NEW DEAL PHASE OF INDIAN REFORM
    A.   Meriam Report
    B.   Reforms under Hoover's administration

Outline, con't.

III. JOHN COLLIER AND THE INDIAN REORGANIZATION ACT
   A. Role and philosophy of Collier in Indian affairs
   B. Passage of the I.R.A.
      1. Major provisions
   C. Critisims of the Indian Reorganization Act
   D. Case study: Application of the I.R.A. to selected tribe(s)

IV. WORLD WAR II AND THE AMERICAN INDIAN
   A. Role of the American Indian in the Armed Services
      1. Ira Hayes
      2. Navajo code talkers
   B. Effects of off-reservation work
   C. Difficulties encountered by returning Indian veterans

V. INDIAN CLAIMS COMMISSION

Points to Emphasize

The National Congress of American Indians was the first non-religious national political organization of Indians (Spicer 1969:143).

Given the option of accepting or rejecting the I.R.A., some tribes voted against it. However, even these tribes received many benefits derived for the Indian New Deal.

Many criticisms leveled against the I.R.A. as similar to those of the New Deal, in general. For example, "it's communistic.""

The Collier administration was an acceleration of reforms begun under the Hoover administration.

One of the reasons for the creation of the Indian Claims Commission "was because it (federal government) saw claims settlement as a necessary step to prepare Indian tribes to manage their own affairs." (Tyler 1974:150)

Activities

Have students debate the pros and cons of the Indian New Deal

In the role of a United States citizen during the New Deal era, have students write a letter to their congressman either in support or against the Wheeler-Howard bill. Include reasons for their opinions.

Discuss the suggestion that had the Wheeler-Howard Act been passed in 1887, the American Indians might by 1934 have been ready for the Dawes Act.

Instructional Aids

Student and Teacher Resources

*Brooking Institution
    1928   Problem of Indian Administration (New York: Johnson Reprint Corp.).

Jackson, Helen Hunt
    1888   A Century of Dishonor (St. Clair Shores, Mich.: Scholarly Press)

*Leupp, Francis
    1910   Indian and His Problem (New York: Johnson Reprint Corp.).

*Lindquist, G.E.
    1923   Red Man in the United States (East Orange, NJ: Thomas Kelly).

UNIT SIXTEEN

Indian Policy After World War II
Termination vs. Self-Determination

Objectives

At the conclusion of this unit, the student will be able to:

Identify:

House Concurrent Resolution 108
National Council of Indian Opportunity
Public Law 280

Evaluate the role of religious organizations in Indian policy--Indian Reorganization
Act and subsequent termination legislation

Describe the arguments for "Freeing the Indians"

Interpret the possible reasons why Dillon Myer was appointed Commissioner of Indian
Affairs

Contrast the philosophy of John Collier and Dillon Myer. Was this change a
reflection of public attitudes?

Compare the role of public sentiment during the I.R.A. and post-World War II
government Indian policy

Describe the tribes' reactions to the above legislation

Appriase the effects of H.C.R. 108 and P.L. 280 on tribal sovereignity

Describe the reaction of the states to P.L. 280. List those states which extended
civil and criminal jurisdiction over Indian reservations within their borders

List those tribes "terminated" by the government

Judge whether tribes really had a choice in accepting termination

Describe tribal reaction to termination

Compare and contrast the economic situation of the Menominee before and after
termination

Identify the major organizations and individuals responsible for denouncing the
government's termination policy

Compare the party platforms twoard American Indians in 1952, 1956, 1960, 1964, 1968,
1972 and 1976.

Outline

I. TERMINATION

    A. Early Proposals
    B. House Concurrent Resolution 108
       1. Tribes terminated
    C. Public Law 280
    D. Case study: The Menominee
    E. Movement for the repeal of H.C.R. 108

II. SELF DETERMINATION

    A. Self-determination and Education Act (Public Law 93-638)

Points to Emphasize

In their resistance to the policy of withdrawing or terminating federal responsibility, the Indian tribes were not expressing a desire to continue indefinitely in a state of dependency, although an obdurate Senator Watkins might make that charge. They would not acknowledge themselves to be dependent in any respect. The protection of their lands and of their right of community control, which outsiders took as evidence of backwardness, was seen by Indians as a contractual relationship not terminable by unilateral decision. (McNickle 1973:113)

The national concern with civil rights in the 1960's expressed in riots, protest marches, court orders and political debates caught up the Indian cause, not always with complete Indian collaboration. Some of the issues involved in the civil rights struggle were not Indian issues. Segregation, which the black man protested so bitterly, was not seen as a denial of social status by Indians. They had never aspired to a place in the white man's society, except as individuals might make that choice for themselves. What Indians as tribal members desired was the good faith performance by the national government of the contractual obligations and reciprocities incorporated in treaties. (McNickle 1973:122)

The legislation establishing the (Indian Claims) commission set a time limit, several times extended, within which tribes might file claims for judgment against the United States. More than 800 such claims have been filed, and during the years 1950-70 awards amounting to about $300 million were paid to 101 tribal claimants. These payments represented less than 5 percent of the amount claimed. (my underline) (McNickle 1973:137)

Activities

Instructional Aids

Films: The Last Menominee (Illinois, Indiana, Oregon)
           ...And the Meek Shall Inherit the Earth (Berkeley, Illinois, Indiana)

Cassette: The Invisible Indian (A-T)
           Self Determination for American Indians: Cultures in Conflict (LL)

Student and Teacher Resources

Daniels, William
     1957   American Indians (New York: H.W. Wilson)

Shames, Deborah ed.
     1972   Freedom with Reservation: The Menominee Struggle to Save Their Land
             and People (Madison: National Committee to Save the Menominee People
             and Forest)

Simpson, George and Milton Yeager
     1959   American Indians and American Life (New York: Russell and Russell)

Taylor, Theodore W.
     1972   The States and Their Indian Citizens (Washington, D.C.: Government
             Printing Office)

The following periodicals frequently contain articles on contemporary Indian
policy:
     Indian Record
     American Indian Journal (of the Institute for the Development of Indian Law)

UNIT SEVENTEEN

Contemporary Indian Society

Objectives

At the conclusion of this unit, the student will be able to:

Identify:

    American Indian Movement
    Dennis Banks
    Chicago Conference: Declaration of Indian Purpose
    National Indian Youth Council
    Rough Rock School
    Relocation program
    Robert Bennett
    Russell Means
    N. Scott Momaday
    Vine DeLoria, Jr.
    National Congress of American Indians
    Red Power
    fish-ins
    Blue Lake
    Indian Education Act of 1972

Describe socioeconomic conditions found on reservations

Compare and contrast the obejctives of the National Congress of American Indians and the American Indian Movement

Compare and contrast the Pan-Indian movement with other minority groups

Evaluate the effects of the Civil Rights movement on the Pan-Indian movement

Describe the more militant episodes of "Red Power": Alcatraz, takeover of the Bureau of Indian Affairs Building, and the occupation of Wounded Knee

Compare and contrast the advantages and disadvantages of living in the city; on the reservation

Outline

    I. INDIANS IN URBAN SOCIETY
        A. Relocation program
        B. Problems encountered by Indians in adjusting to city life
        C. Reasons for migration back to the reservations
        D. Formal and informal associations in the city

Outline, con't.

II. PAN-INDIANISM: INDIAN RESPONSES TO GOVERNMENT POLICIES

    A. Passive
    B. Active
        1. Militant
            a. Takeover of Alcatraz
            b. Seizure of the B.I.A. headquarters
            c. Wounded Knee
    C. Indian organizations
        1. American Indian Movement
        2. National Congress of American Indians
        3. National Indian Youth Council

III. MODERN RESERVATION LIFE

    A. Survey of reservation conditions
        1. Housing
        2. Health
        3. Employment
    B. Economic development
    C. Legal questions
        1. Taxation
        2. Water rights
        3. Hunting and fishing rights
        4. Treaty rights

IV. INDIAN EDUCATION

    A. Reservation schools
        1. Rough Rock
    B. Boarding schools
    C. Indian students in public schools
    D. Indians in textbooks

Points to Emphasize

Activities

Oral or written reports on selected topics on contemporary Indian society (see
  es 104-105).

Student survey on the role of Indians in history textbooks used in classrooms

Discussion group on the adjustments Indians must make to city life when moving
 from a reservation

Show films depicting Indian life on two different Indian reservations, i.e., the
Navajo and the Pine Rige reservations and have studnets discuss and compare
contemporary Indian reservation life

Instructional Aids

Films: Act Now (American Indian Policy Review Commission)
            Way of Our Fathers (Indian Education) (Berkeley)
            Where Has the Warrior Gone? (Illinois)
            Navajos of the 1970's (Illinois)
            Broken Treaty at Battle Mountain (Soho Cinema, Ltd.)
            Our Vanishing Wilderness: The Water is So Clear That A Blind Man
                Could See (Blue Lake) (Indiana, Illinois)
            The Pride and the Shame (Time-Life, Minnesota)
            Navajo: The Last Red Indians (Time-Life)
            The American Indian Speaks (EBEC, Illinois)
            The Exiles (McGraw-Hill, Indiana, Oregon)
            Treaties Made, Treaties Broken (Fish-ins) (Berkeley, Minnesota, Illinois,
                Indiana, Oregon, McGraw-Hill)
            Lament of the Reservation (Berkeley, Minnesota, Illinois, Indiana,
                Oregon, McGraw-Hill)
            Indians of the Plains: Present-Day Life (Minnesota)
            The Forgotten American (Minnesota, Berkeley, Oregon)
            Forty-seven Cents (California Indians and Their Claims case) (Berkeley)
            Indians and Chiefs (urban Indians) (Berkeley)
            Little White Salmon Indian Settlement (Fish-ins) (Berkeley, Oregon, T-C)
            The Dispossessed (Berkeley)
            The Hopi Way (Black Mesa) (F-I)
            Black Coal, Red Power (Black Mesa) (Berkeley, Indiana)
            The Navajo: A Study in Cultural Contrast (Indiana)
            Indian Mainstream (Berkeley)
            A Song for Dead Warriors(Wounded Knee) (T-C)
            Ten Thousand Beads for Navajo Sam (urban Indians) (Indiana, Berkeley)
            Why Did Gloria Die? (reservation life) (Indiana)
            Look What We Have Done to This Land (Pyramid)

Filmstrips: The Indians vs. the Giant Utilities: Whose Values Prevail at
(sound)   Black Mesa (Inquiry)
            Powers of My Spirit: The American Indian (Inquiry)
            The First Americans (Pan-Indianism) (SSSS)
            The Navajo Indian (RMI)
            The Apache Indian (RMI)
            The American Indian: A Dispossessed People (GA)

Cassette: Wounded Knee and After (A-T)
            Trial by Prejudice (A-T)
            Black Mesa: A Tragedy (A-T)
            Today's Indian War (A-T)
            From Alcatraz to Chicago (A-T)
            The Bureau of Indian Affairs (A-T)
            The Angry Indians (American Indian Chicago Conference, 1961) (LL)
            A Voice of the American Indian (LL)
            The Renaissance of the American Indian (LL)

Student and Teacher Resources

American Friends Service Committee
    1970   Uncommon Controversy: Fishing Rights to the Muckleshoot, Puyallup,
            and Nisqually Indians (Seattle: University of Washington Press).

Blue Cloud, Peter
    1973   Alcatraz is Not an Island (Berkeley, CA: Wingbow Press).

Brophy, William A. and Sophie D. Aberle
    1969   Indian: America's Unfinished Business, Report of the Commission on the
            Rights, Liberties, and Responsibilities of the American Indian (Norman:
            University of Oklahoma Press).

Burnette, Robert
    1971   Tortured Americans (Englewood Cliffs, NJ: Prentice-Hall, Inc.).

Burnette, Robert and John Koster
    1974   The Road to Wounded Knee (New York: Bantam Books, Inc.).

Cahn, Edgar S. ed.
    1969   Our Brother's Keeper: The Indian in White America (New York: New
            American Library).

Costo, Rupert, ed.
    1969   Textbooks and the American Indian (San Francisco: Indian Historian
            Press).

De La Garza, Rudolph, et. al.
    1973   Chicanos and Native Americans: The Territorial Minorities (Englewood
            Cliffs, NJ: Prentice-Hall, Inc.).

DeLoria, Vine, Jr.
    1970   We Talk, You Listen (New York: Macmillan Publishing Co., Inc.).

    1973   God Is Red (New York: Grosset and Dunlop, Inc.).

    1974   Behind the Trail of Broken Treaties (New York: Delacorte Press).

Friar, Ralph and Natasha Friar
    1973   The Only Good Indian....the Hollywood Gospel (New York: Drama Book
            Specialists Publishers).

Fuchs, Estelle and Robert Havighurst
    1972   To Live on This Earth: American Indian Education (Garden City, New
            York: Doubleday and Co., Inc.).

Gridley, Marion E.
    1972   Contemporary American Indian Leaders (New York: Dodd, Mead and Co.).

Henry, Jeannette ed.
    1972   The American Indian Reader: Education (San Francisco: Indian Historian
            Press).

    1974   The American Indian Reader: Current Affairs (San Francisco: Indian
            Historian Press).

Student and Teacher Resources, con't.

    1974   Indian Voices: The Native American Today (San Francisco: Indian Historian Press).

Hertzberg, Hazel W.
    1971   Search for an American Indian Identity: Modern Pan-Indian Movements (New York: Syracuse University Press).

Jones, Louis T.
    1972   Amerindian Education (San Antonio, Tex.: Naylor, Co.).

Josephy, Alvin M., Jr.
    1971   Red Power: The American Indians' Fight for Freedom (New York: McGraw-Hill Book Co.).

Kickingbird, Kirke and Karen Duchencaus
    1973   One Hundred Million Acres (New York: Macmillan Publishing Co.).

Levine, Stuart and Nancy O. Lurie eds.
    1968   American Indian Today (Baltimore, Md.: Penguin Books, Inc.).

Levitan, Sar A. and Barbara Hetrick
    1971   Big Brother's Indian Programs-with Reservations (New York: McGraw-Hill Book Co.).

Levitan, Sar A. and William B. Johnston
    1975   Indian Giving: Federal Programs for Native Americans (Baltimore: Johns Hopkins University Press).

Marquis, Arnold
    1974   A Guide to America's Indians: Ceremonies, Reservations, and Museums (Norman: University of Oklahoma Press).

Marriott, Alice and Carol K. Rachlin
    1971   Peyote (New York: New American Library)

Marx, Herbert L., Jr., ed.
    1973   The American Indian: A Rising Ethnic Force (New York: H.W. Wilson)

Meyer, William
    1971   Native Americans: The New Indian Resistance (New York: International Publishing Co., Inc.).

Nurge, Ethel
    1970   Modern Sioux: Social Systems and Reservation Culture (Lincoln: University of Nebraska Press).

Shorris, Earl
    1974   The Death of the Great Spirit (New York: New American Library)

*Slotkin, James S.
    1956   The Peyote Religion: A Study in Indian-White Relations (Glencoe, Ill.: Free Press).

Student and Teacher Resources, con't.

*Sorkin, Alan
    1971   American Indians and Federal Aid (Washington, D.C.: Brookings Institute).

*Spicer, Edward H.
    1961   Perspectives in American Indian Culture Change (Chicago: University
            of Chicago Press).

Steiner, Stan
    1969   New Indians (New York: Dell Publishing).

Szasz, Margaret
    1974   Education and the American Indian, 1928-1973: The Road to Self
            Determination (Albuquerque: University of New Mexico Press).

Waddell, Jack O. and Michael O. Watson
    1971   The American Indian in Urban Society (Waltham, Mass.: Little, Brown
            and Co.).

*Walker, Deward E., Jr. ed.
    1972   The Emergent Native Americans: A Reader in Cultural Contact (Waltham,
            Mass.: Little, Brown and Co.).

Waters, Frank
    1971   Man Who Killed the Deer (Chicago, Ill.: Swallow Press).

Wilson, Edmund
    1970   Apologies to the Iroquois (Westminster, Md.: Random House, Inc.).

The following periodicals frequently contain articles on contemporary Indian affairs:

    Human Organization
    Indian Historian
    Wassaja (newspaper)
    Akwesasne Notes (newspaper)
    Civil Rights Digest
    Journal of American Indian Education

FINAL PAPER

The United States and the North American Indian

LENGTH: 5 to 7 typewritten pages
SOURCES: You must use at least 5 different sources (textbooks not included)
TOPICS: Your choice of a topic should focus on events and/or personalities since
      the turn of the century, in the area of American Indian history of literature
SUGGESTED TOPICS:

Federal Policy

Bursum Bill (1922)
Indian Citizenship Act (June 2, 1924)
Indian Reorganization Act (1934)
   John Collier
Johnson-O'Malley Act (1934)
Indian Claim Commission (1946)
Public Law 280 (1953)
Termination Legislation
   Menominee
   Klamath
Relocation Program
Bureau of Indian Affairs
Indian Health Division of H.E.W. (1955)

Personalities

Charles Curtis (Government)
Charles Bender (Sports)
Louis Tewaniwa (Sports)
Jim Thorpe (Sports)
Anne Dodge Wauneka (Tribal Government)
Maria Martinez (Art)
Vine DeLoria, Jr. (Lawyer, writer)
Billy Mills (Sports)
N. Scott Momaday (Writer)
Robert Bruce (Government)
Edward P. Dozier (Anthropologist)
D'Arcy McNickle (Anthropologist, writer)
Buffe Saint-Marie (Music)
Frank Waters (Writer)

Pan Indianism

National Congress of American Indians
American Indian Movement
National Indian Youth Council
"Red Power"
Taos-Blue Lake
Alcatraz
Wounded Knee II
Occupation of B.I.A. Building
Black Mesa

<u>Final Paper Topics</u>, con't.

<u>Education</u>

Navajo Community College
Ramah Elementary School

<u>Indian Health</u>

Suicide
Alcoholism
Disease

Indians' role in World War I, World War II, Korean and Vietnam War:
    Ira Hayes
    Navajo Code Talkers

Compare/contrast major novels by leading American Indian writers.

Image of American Indian in media.

Reservation life: focus on a specific reservation or compare life on two different reservations.

Indians in Urban Society: Focus on Indians in a particular city or problem.

Native American experience in California
Native American experience in San Bernardino County

American Indian law

Any current event happening in upcoming semester.

APPENDIX

List of distributors for instructional aids
Suggested diagnostic and summative evaluations

Distributors

American Indian Policy Review Commission
    House Office Building
    Annex 2
    Second and D Streets, SW
    Washington, D.C. 20515

Association of American Geography (AAG)
    1710 16th Street NW
    Washington, D.C. 20009

The Center for Cassette Studies (A-T)
    Audio-Text Cassettes
    8110 Webb Avenue
    North Hollywood, California 91605

The Baker and Taylor Company
    Audio Visual Services Division
    P.O. Box 23
    Momence, Illinois 60954

Department of Interior
    Bureau of Indian Affairs
    Washington, D.C. 20245

Cassettes Unlimited (CU)
    Roanake, Texas 76262

Civic Education Service (CES)
    1725 K Street, NW
    Suite 1009
    Washington, D.C. 20006

Current Affairs (CA)
    24 Danbury Road
    Walton, Connecticut 06897

Education Audio Visual, Inc. (EAV)
    P.O. Box 538
    El Toro, California 92630

Distributors, con't.

Educational Development Corporation (EDC)
     P.O. Drawer 5500
     Lakeland, Florida 33803

Educational Media, Inc. (EMI)
     P.O. Box 39
     809 Industrial Way
     Ellensburg, Washington 98926

Films Incorporated
     1144 Wilmette Avenue
     Wilmette, Illinois 60091

Fitzhenry and Whiteside (FW)
     150 Lesmill Road
     Don Mills, Ontario M3B 2T5

Folkways Records and Service Corporation
     701 7th Avenue
     New York, New York

Guidance Associates (GA)
     757 Third Avenue
     New York, New York 10017

Hamond Incorporated
     Maplewood, New Jersey 07040

Indiana University
     Audio Visual Center
     Bloomington, Indiana 47401

Inquiry Audio Visuals
     1754 West Farragut Avenue
     Chicago, Illinois 60640

Learning Films, Ltd.
     Secondari Productions
     745 Fifth Avenue
     New York, New York 10022

Listening Library, Inc. (LL)
     1 Park Avenue
     Old Greenwich, Connecticut 06870

Macmillan Films (Mac)
     34 MacQuesten Parkway South
     Nt. Vernon, New York 10550

McGraw-Hill
     Office of Multi-Ethnic Services
     1221 Avenue of the Americas
     New York, New York 10020

Distributors, con't.

Mankind Publishing Company (MFR)
    8060 Melrose Avenue
    Los Angeles, California 90046

Modern Film Rentals
    2323 New Hyde Park Road
    New Hyde Park, New York 11040

Multi-Media Productions, Inc. (M-M)
    P.O. Box 5097
    Stanford, California 94305

National Geographic Society (NGS)
    National Geographic Educational Services
    Department 76
    Washington, D.C. 20036

A.J. Nystrom and Company
    3333 Elston Avenue
    Chicago, Illinois 60618

Oregon Division of Continuing Education
    Oregon State System of Higher Education
    Film Library
    1633 Southwest Park Avenue
    P.O. Box 1491
    Portland, Oregon 97207

The Perfection Form Company (PF)
    1000 North Second Avenue
    Logan, Iowa 51546

Prentice-Hall Media (P-H)
    Department B
    150 White Plains Road
    Tarrytown, New York 10591

Pyramid Films
    P.O. Box 1048
    Santa Monica, California 90406

RMI Educational Films, Inc.
    701 Westport Road
    Kansas City, Missouri 64111

Schloat Productions
    150 White Plains Road
    Tarrytown, New York 10591

Scholastic Book Services
    904 Sylvan Avenue
    Englewood Cliffs, New York 07632

Distributors, con't.

Social Studies School Service (SSSS)
     10,000 Culver Blvd.
     Culver City, California 90230

Soho Cinema, Ltd.
     225 Lafayette Street
     New York, New York 10012

Southwest Film Center (SW Film Center)
     169 Franklin Avenue
     San Gabriel, California 91775

Time-Life Films
     43 West 16th Street
     New York, New York 10001

Tri-Continental Films Center (T-C)
     P.O. Box 4430
     Berkeley, California 94704

University of California
     Extension Media Center
     Berkeley, California 94720

University of Minnesota
     A.V. Library Service
     Continuing Education and Extension
     3300 University Avenue Southeast
     Minneapolis, Minnesota 55414

Valiant Instructional Material Corporation
     195 Bonhomme Street
     Hockenberg, New York 07602

Walt Disney Educational Media Company
     800 Sonora Avenue
     Glendale, California 91201

Xerox Education Publications
     245 Long Hill Road
     Middletown, Connecticut 06457

Suggested Summative Evaluation Questions (Exam on American Indian Cultures)

I. Definitions: 2 points each; total possible points - 20. Choose 5 terms from Column A and 5 from Column B and define them in five to seven sentences. Use your own wording.

Column A
"Indian"
Pine Tree Chiefs
Council of Fifty
Orenda
Miko
"Red towns"
Great Sun
False Face Society
Grand Medicine Society
Calumet
Dream Festival
Green Corn Ceremony
"wigwam"
Manitou

Column B
Bering Land Bridge
Vision Quest
"Old Settlers"
Coup
Mogollom
Potlatch
Totem Pole
Sun Dance
Give Away Feast
Basketmakers
Kachina
Dene
"Mission" Indians
Kit Foxes Society

II. Compare and contrast one of the tribal pairs in terms of (1) material culture (2) subsistence patterns, (3) political and social organization, (4) religion, and (5) settlement patterns. (15 possible points)

    A.   Iroquois-Natchez
    B.   Creek-Penobscot (Algonquians of Eastern woodlands)
    C.   Sioux-Zuni
    D.   Pima-Sioux
    E.   Yuma-Paiute (Great Basin)
    F.   Nootka (Northwest Coast)-Nez Perce (Plateau)
    G.   Objibwa-Cree
    H.   Any two of your choice with approval of instructor

III. Contrast American Indian attitudes, traditions and values with those of the Euro-American in two of the following areas. (15 possible points)

    A.   Government
    B.   Property: Land Tenure
    C.   Religion
    D.   Social organization
    E.   Social identification

Mid Term-50 points.

I. Identification-Answer any 5 of the following: (5 points each)

   A. King Philip   F. Handsome Lake
   B. Pope   G. John Ross
   C. Tecumseh   H. Sand Creek Massacre
   D. Alexander McGillivray I. Cheif Joseph
   E. Twenskwatawa   J. Cherokee Nation vs. Georgia/Worcester vs.
                                                   Georgia

II. Essay-Answer only one of the following questions: (25 points each)

   A. Summarize the relations of one of the following tribes with the Europeans
   and later the Americans from early contact to the 1830's-1840's: Iroquois,
   Eastern Algonquins, Pueblos, or one fo the Five Civilized Tribes-Cherokees,
   Creeks, Choctaws, Chickasaws, Seminoles.

   B. Francis Parkman in his study of "The Jesuits of North America" wrote,
   "Spanish civilization crushed the Indian; English civilization scorned and
   neglected him; French civilization embraced and cherished him." Support
   (or criticize) this viewpoint. Include in your answer (1) the motives which
   account for the differences in colonial attitudes and policies toward the
   American Indian; (2) Indian response to these policies; and (3) a comparison
   of the Spanish, English, and French policies toward the Indian in the following areas: intermarriage, trade and approach to land cessions.

   C. Summarize the effects of the American Revolution on the American Indian
   and his aspirations of striking a balance with the Europeans' powers. Include in your answer (1) the role of the Indian in the American REvolution;
   (2) effects of the Revolution on intertribal and intratribal relations; (3)
   Indian response to the Treaty of Paris (1783); and (4) the immediate effect
   of their (the Indian's) defeat on early United States government Indian policy.

   D. "The President's (Jackson) justification of Indian removal was the one
   usually applied to the displacement of the Indians by newer Americans-the
   superiority of a farming culture to a hunting culture, and of Anglo-American
   'liberty, civilization and religion' to the strange and barbarous way of the
   red man," writes Mary Young in her article on "Indian Removal and Land
   Allotment: The Civilized Tribes and Jacksonian Justice." This rationalization,
   however, became invalid when applied to the Indians of the Southeast. Using
   the Cherokees as an example, (1) explain the invalidity of Jackson's rationalization for displacing the Indian; (2) summarize the internal changes in
   Cherokee society as a result of the "Cherokee Renaissance;" and (3) intratribal
   response to removal.

   E. Ewer's "The Indian Trade of the Upper Missouri before Lewis and Clark,"
   presents the reader with a look at Indian-Indian relations on the Plains
   focusing on trade relationships. Describe the aboriginal trade, i.e., types of
   goods exchanged, participating tribes, flow of goods. What effects did white
   traders and their goods have on the aboriginal trade pattern? What effects
   did later American encroachment and warfare have on these trade relationships?

Mid Term

Cultural Background

I. Identification: Choose any 6 of the following terms and define them in 3 to 5 sentences (5 points each)

"Indian"	potlatch	Miko
crenda	coup	totem pole
Council of Fifty	"Old Settlers"	Shoshonean
Great Sun	Sun Dance	
Beloved Men	"Mission Indians"	
katchina	calumet	

II. Essay: Compare and contrast one of the tribal pairs in terms of (1) material culture, (2) subsistence patterns, (3) political and social organization, (4) religion, and (5) settlement patterns. (35 points)

Tribal Pairs

A. Iroquois-Natchez
B. Creek-Penobscot (Algonquins of the Eastern Woodlands)
C. Sioux-Zuni
D. Yuma-Paiute
E. Nootka (Northwest Coast)-Nez Perce (Plateau)
F. Objibwa-Cree

Historical Material (Total 35 points possible)

I. Identification: Choose any 4 of the following terms/names and define them in 3 to 5 sentences (5 points each)

John Eliot	Tenskwatawa
King Philip	Seminole Wars
Pope	John Ross
Tecumseh	Wocester vs. Georgia
Treaty of Hopewell	"Trail of Tears"
Alexander McGillivray	Powhatan Confederacy

II. Essay: Choose one of the following questions to answer: (15 points possible)

1. Describe the legal and moral justifications used to dispossess the Indian of his lands. Criticize their validity in light of the readings and discussions on American Indian cultures.

2. What effects did white contact have on Indian-Indian relations? Give at least two examples.

3. Compare and contrast colonial policies and attitudes toward the American Indian.

4. Choose one of the following tribes and summarize their relations with the Euro-American: Iroquois, Cherokees, Creeks or Algonquians.

5. The main thrust of early Indian policy was to "civilize the Indian." Describe the objectives and methods of these early attempts to bring "civilization" to the Indians.

1. Evaluate early relations between Indians and European explorers and colonists. Include how Indians viewed the Europeans.

2. The major realm of adaptation of Indian tribes in contact with whites from 1540-1794 was political. Support this statement using as an example either the Iroquois, Creek or Eastern Algonquian tribes. Compare and contrast the three to some degree in your answer.

3. Describe the role of "displaced persons" focusing on one of the following tribes: Shawnee, Delaware, or Tuscarora.

4. Compare and contrast Handsome Lake and his teachings with the Algonquian prophets (Delaware prophet and Tenskwatawa).

5. Compare and contrast colonial policies toward the American Indians by the French, Spanish and British. Include in your answer Indian diplomacy toward the colonial powers. To what degree was it successful?

6. Summarize the weaknesses of government Indian policy under the Articles of Confederation and as a consequence, power(s) granted to the federal government under the Constitution.

Differentiate the specific roles of each branch (legislative, executive and judicial) of the U.S. governemnt in the area of Indian policy.

7. Evaluate the role of the Indian in the Revolutionary War. Include reasons the Indian tended to ally with the British. What direction did the diplomacy of the colonies take to counteract?

8. Identify the important factors and individuals in Cherokee development during their cultural renaissance and describe their ramifications on Cherokee society.

9. Reconstruct the series of events leading up to Cherokee removal and then describe the removal itself.

10. Describe the adjustments and reactions made by the Creeks after removal in terms of thier own society and in their relationships with other tribes.

_____

I. One criticism leveled against Federal Indian policy is its inconsistency. Spicer writes, "During the century from the 1860's to the 1960's there were two peaks in Congressional action based on dominance of the view that the special governmental relationship should be severed. There were also two peaks based on the opposing view that it should continue." Identify the major piece(s) of Congressional legislation in those four peaks. Compare and contrast them in terms of their basic philosophy, how both whites and Indians reacted, and finally their effects upon the Indian community. (50 points)

II. Choose any two of the following questions: (25 points each)

    A. Pan Indianism: The emergence of Indian activism during the 1960's and 1970's was one of the responses to the detrimental effects of termination legislation. Day distinguishes two broad types of tactics: obstructive and facilitative. Compare the two forms.

B.   American Indians in Urban Society: Today over 50% of the American Indian population lives in urban areas. What leads Indian individuals to the city? Once there, what are some fo the adjustments and adaptations made by the individual? Compare and contrast the advantages of living on and off the reservation?

C.   Indian Education: Virgil Vogel lists four methods used to create false impressions toward the American Indian. Identify two of them and evaluate how they might lead to a negative self-concept in the Indian child.

D.   Tribal and Reservation Life: (either a or b)

a.   In recent years the dramatic increase in Indian suicide rate has become a major source of concern. Identify several of the motives especially those resulting from Indian-white contact.

b.   Summarize the major premises in one of the following: American Indian drinking; Transculturalization; Health practices.

I.   Identification: Choose any 5 of the names/terms below and identify them in 5 to 10 sentences.

a.   Sand Creek Massacre   e.   peyote cult
b.   Chief Joseph   f.   relocation program
c.   Wovoka/Ghost Dance   g.   Indian Claims Commission
d.   Meriam report   h.   Sitting Bull

II. Essay: Choose one of the following essay questions to answer:

A.   Indians in Urban Society-Today, over 50% of the Indian population reside in urban centers. Why are Indians moving to the cities? Once there, what adjustments do Indians have to make to "city life"? Why are many returning to the reservations despite the increased opportunities, economic and otherwise, found in cities?

B.   Self-determination-Summarize the major findings and recommendations in President Nixon's statement on Indian Self-determination. In light of assigned reading and the oral reports, do you feel his answers to the "Indian problem" are viable?

C.   Pan-Indianism-Take one of the following examples of the more militant aspects of "Red Power" and summarize the events leading up to it and the final outocme fo the takeover: Alcatraz, Takeover of the B.I.A. Building, or Wounded Knee Occupation.

D.   Modern Reservation Life-Describe conditions found on most reservations today: economic, housing, health conditions, etc. What sort of improvements are being made or planned in these areas?